LOVE IS ALWAYS THE LESSON

My Stories from the Edge

Sherry Smith R.N.N.P.

Love Is Always the Lesson: My Stories from the Edge
Sherry Smith R.N.N.P.

This book was printed in the United States of America.
First Edition June 2018
To order additional copies of this book contact: Amazon/Kindle.com

Praise for *Love Is Always the Lesson*

"In *Love Is Always the Lesson,* Sherry vulnerably shares some traumatic experiences in love and loss that she's faced in her life in order to reveal how they transformed her awareness that love survives the physical death of the body and that real and very present spiritual energies wrap us in love and guidance. In bypassing the voice of her ego to share very private aspects of her life, Sherry helps us see that life's challenges can bring tremendous spiritual growth and that we are not alone in facing the inevitable struggles in our lives.

Her lessons give us hope, encouragement and a warm pat on the back in thinking about our own life's obstacles. You will feel a renewed sense of insight in embracing your journey knowing that your inevitable lessons will give you a stronger ability to contribute to the greater good. *Love Is Always the Lesson* is ultimately an uplifting book and Sherry's message of love will stay with you for a long time."

Allyson Cain
Pain patient

"Love Is Always the Lesson - How true! I have just finished reading this touching memoir by Sherry Smith. I felt honored to be invited into such a truly compelling account of a life which has been lived so richly in love. Sherry takes the reader on an emotional rollercoaster ride as she recalls the trials and turmoil that she has experienced over her life time.

There are many aspects to the book, and it manages to reach a wide audience covering many real life-issues - some will leave the reader beguiled but always bringing the focus back to a life story built on deep faith and love."

Daniella R.

PREFACE

Allow me to introduce myself. My name is Sherry Smith and by profession I am a Registered Nurse, Nurse Practitioner. I was born to young parents in 1951. During my formative years, my family resided on a large turkey ranch in the Central San Joaquin Valley of California. It was a humble existence with work, church, and family being the center of our world. Even as a small child, I can recall having an interest and acceptance of mystical experiences.

Our family eventually relocated to Washington state where I became a registered nurse in 1971. As far back as I can remember, I planned to be a nurse. Being the oldest of four children, I was groomed to be a caretaker. I have always found caring for others to be immensely gratifying.

In 1974, I completed nurse practitioner training in Los Angeles. My field of study was women's health care. That same year, I married the gynecologist I was working for. We shared the specialty practice until his untimely death in 1981. I truly enjoyed caring for women during their pregnancies and addressing their gynecology issues. It was an honor to support them during these intimate times.

Along with my dedication to caring for women, I was quite interested in holistic medicine. I would always consider the bigger picture of what was going on in my patient's lives. I was sincerely interested in the psycho-social issues regarding family, work, and marriage.

In my research, I began to be aware of energy as it related to health. I have attended cutting edge seminars on topics such as quantum physics and energy medicine. I was trained in Therapeutic Touch, an energy technique taught to nurses. A number of other nurses, including myself, learned to balance the energy field in order to enhance the body's ability to heal itself and reduce pain.

Over the years, I became more aware of patient's issues surrounding death and loss. Being the curious type, I would inquire of any unusual experiences. Patients were often eager to share their interesting stories. I also counseled them on grief and recovery from loss.

At age thirty, I had my own very vivid metaphysical experiences. This was a result of the death of my husband and was the beginning of my spiritual awakening. While I haven't seen anything resembling a flying saucer, I have been profoundly surprised and excited by the things I have witnessed and heard. I fully realize that my exposure and subsequent assumptions defy conventional wisdom.

The next chapter of my life brought a complicated marital relationship further challenging me spiritually. The presence of love sustained me through the storms of this passionate yet difficult journey. Due to my belief in the power of commitment, I stubbornly refused to break up our family.

To talk about death without an overview of the life that preceded it would be incomplete. I fully realize it's a whopper of a tale! Perceptions often change over time, yet universal truth stands alone. It has been my privilege to utilize my life experiences in support of others during their transition times.

For years, I have been encouraged to share some of my transpersonal stories. I found myself feeling quite vulnerable at the thought of revealing these most private and sacred encounters. None-the-less, I have reached an age where adding my experiences to the body of evidence that already exists is more important than my ego anxiety.

Scribing my stories reminded me of a dream I had many years ago: *I was running through a bazaar feeling free as a bird. I looked down and realized I was naked and totally exposed!* In writing this, I have worked through the layers of my vulnerability. I decided to adopt an attitude of determination and one of a willingness to be known by others.

With gratitude, I eagerly anticipate the freedom that only letting go can provide. I am honored that you are taking this journey with me.

Sincerely,
Sherry Smith R.N.N.P.

I welcome your comments and questions.
I am interested in hearing your sacred stories.
Please email me: sherrysmith51@aol.com

Acknowledgements

My heartfelt gratitude to all who have walked with me and for the support of my husband, family, friends, angels, guides, and healers. The lessons of love I have received from each and every one of you has sustained me throughout some very dark and confusing times. I cherish the joy shared as well. A special thank you for all the pearls you have tossed my way. Your encouragement, as well as your total belief in my ability to grow and stand tall, has been a constant source of light on my path. I am able to embrace my journey more fully because of your gifts. You are the *rainbow* of my life. ~Sherry

Dedication

This book is dedicated to my daughter Alysia. I am uplifted by your constant support and love. You have shared both my joys and sorrows. Thank you for believing in me, for being my soulmate, and for choosing me as your mother. I am grateful for your courage and curiosity to tiptoe to the edge. I thank *God* every day for the wonder of you. ~Your Momma

Love is light …
Truth is simple …
Be the light …

CONTENTS

PART THREE

PART ONE

CHAPTER 1

The Journey: An Overview

Love in its essence is spiritual fire.

~Lucius Annaeus Seneca

This is a collection of stories about love, loss, and learning. It is my belief that by sharing our experiences we can help prepare each other for life's greatest challenges. The last chapter of life provides the springboard from which we journey to the next world. Standing on the edge of this life, as a loved one transitions to the other side, can be a watershed experience thus providing the basic conditions for transformation and spiritual realization.

Through love's intention, a connection exists. Spirits convey an eagerness to share an enlightened perspective of their life on earth and sometimes seem astonished at their current glorious reality. This information can be profound. I believe these heartwarming and cherished encounters are often available to those who choose to listen for the whispers.

As a tribute to love's presence, we can choose to assign *higher* meaning to the challenging circumstances we face. It takes courage to relive the darkest days of our lives, yet the past often has much to teach us. Understanding our journey can be transformative and lead to a better tomorrow. Listening to love's reassuring message is the path to the healing miracle we seek.

A Course in Miracles (Foundation for Inner Peace) teaches that nothing real can be threatened, and love is the only thing that is real. Our legacy of love is certainly all that survives death. I trust these stories provide evidence of a continuation of life and an ability to communicate from the next level of existence.

When we experience loss, the willingness to grieve the many dreams we must release is critical to our well-being. The courage to do this emotional work and move on is an important opportunity for strengthening our *authentic self.* An openness to guidance and spiritual healing is a gift available to all. As our loved one takes passage into their new existence, we can choose to embrace a fresh beginning for ourselves. Join me, as I take you on my spiritual voyage, imparting these sacred stories as my offering.

I was given this dream many years ago: *I am laboring, fervently weaving with threads of many colors onto a large heavy fabric. It is stretched on a frame in front of me. My fingers are sore and stiff. My body is aching from the fatigue of the tedious project. I am feeling quite frustrated because the result looks like a confused, disorganized, and pattern-less display of many colors. There are varying textures and lengths of threads. Truly, it looks a mess! At this point, a presence speaks to me: "Child, I will show you the life you have created." The frame is turned over. I gasp at the incredibly beautiful tapestry. It is an intricate and lovely perspective of my life. The vividness and clarity of each scene speaks for itself. There is at once an understanding of the journey I am on, the mystery of life, and how we are shielded from seeing the full beauty and continuity until the last thread is woven.* This is the teaching of the dream.

CHAPTER 2

First Love ... First Death

Love is how you stay alive even after you are gone.

~ Unknown

In the quiet of the early morning, as I set my intentions for the day, I often find myself highly receptive to unusual thoughts. I feel the comfort of the supporting energy of love. The whispers of departed loved ones guide and remind me of their presence. I've chronicled messages, stories, and dreams throughout my journey. This has helped bring awareness of my spiritual evolution.

When revisiting the past, I often find a memory will surface. This is followed by emotions I did not allow myself the luxury to feel or express at the time. An honest reflection has the potential to bring much needed release and its resulting emotional balance. With hindsight, comes insight and healing. This has given me the gift of understanding the past and the ability to embrace the joyfulness of the present.

I assume most of us remember our first surreal experience with human death. I can still see my small six-year-old self ... standing by a pink metal casket and holding my spirited grandmother's hand. She believed that taking me to see my first dead body would be educational. The deceased was Aunt Josie who reached her late nineties before death caught up with her. She was my grandmother's cousin and had died of natural causes.

Aunt Josie's perfectly coiffed hair rested on a silk, lacy white pillow. She was dressed in her finest attire. To a young child she was an eerie sight. As we gazed upon her shriveled body, I was acutely aware of the heavy floral aroma and the lingering, odd scent of embalming fluid. My grandmother said to me softly but to my surprise, "Touch her."

At this point, the room began to spin. As I swooned, I braced myself against the hard casket and hesitated. She took my tiny fingers and laid them upon Aunt Josie's cold and very dead hand. She explained to me that even though she looked as if she were asleep, she was dead and had gone to be with *God*. It was clear to me that whatever life had inhabited her body had moved on to this mystical place my grandmother called Heaven.

I marvel at my grandmother's wisdom in exposing me to death in what she believed was an unemotional situation. It proved to be a perfect teaching moment. She knew that death could come into our lives at the most unexpected times. This was her way of preparing me for the hardest part of life, the part where we say goodbye.

This was the first of many funerals and viewings to which she would take me. Over the years, I became her official funeral companion. Between the moments of hushed tones and whispers, we respectfully told stories of the deceased. I especially enjoyed the fellowship of friends and family reuniting to comfort each other and honor the deceased. I came to understand that this demonstrated the survival skills of those left behind.

Today, I realize the extent of my grandparents' unconditional love for me. During my childhood, they were my constant companions. Through their love and care, I learned about life, death, and most importantly about *God*. When I was sixteen, on a car trip with my grandfather, I had a profound expanded spiritual awareness of the connection of our two souls. I was cognizant of a union with him that I can only describe as agape' (the highest form of love). His demonstration of selfless love served as a mirror to remind me that I too was created in *God's* image.

My most touching experience of death, with my grandmother, was my grandfather's funeral. He had succumbed to a devastating illness. We sat in the family viewing room which was separated from the other mourners by a white veiled curtain. This tradition afforded the family privacy at such a vulnerable time. As usual, she handed me a floral, scented handkerchief to wipe my tears. This gesture brought me great comfort. She held my hand gently, and we wept together for the man we both loved so deeply.

There was an awareness that the profound emotions being expressed were very cleansing.

I distinctly remember my heart speaking to me. My grandfather whispered, "*I will always truly love you*." My pain was replaced with the healing energy of unconditional love. I knew in that moment that he would live in my heart forever. Our love had no beginning, and now I knew it had no end. This understanding of unconditional love is the safety net which allows me to love without fear of loss.

Through many profound experiences, I have come to know death as merely a doorway to the next adventure. I have always been curious and inquisitive regarding the mystery of death and the resulting changes it brings. This has provided me with rich opportunities for growth and a rebirthing time of my own. For me, the most important takeaways have been; Life is eternal … Sorrow is not forever … *Love is*.

CHAPTER 3

Life Gets Messy

***Be joyous and celebrate love
wherever it beckons you.***

~Emmanuel's Book

Traumatic events are hard-wired into our brains. We can pull out the memories and replay them as if they happened yesterday. I play this one in technicolor every Fourth of July. I have no choice in the matter. I wake up and before my head is off the pillow, I begin to remember the last precious day with my first love.

Before I replay the memory of that day, permit me to take you to the beginning of this fated life. I share the abbreviated version of my early lessons with romantic love:

I was nineteen, enjoying the freedom of being a single student nurse in the second year of my training. I had a vision of a strong and independent life. Even so, I already had a head start on giving up my authenticity. Addiction had deeply affected my family of origin. I did not understand the influence this was having on my hunger for love. I mistakenly believed you gave up yourself for someone else's love and acceptance. Missing, was the strength of character needed to handle the ensuing moral crises.

It was the first class after lunch. I often fought drowsiness from my mid-day meal, but today I felt an unusual energy as a guest speaker sauntered into the room. I distinctly remember where I was sitting in that tiered lecture hall. He was an attractive doctor whose specialty was Obstetrics and Gynecology. I had no idea who he was. Dr. James Scott, I was told. I felt like I was hit by a lightning bolt. I began to quiver, and I felt flushed.

I didn't hear a word the doctor said. I turned to my friend next to me and whispered, "I am going to marry that man."

She laughed and whispered back, "He's married and has four kids." She worked in his clinic and knew him. I dismissed the entire fantasy but was totally mesmerized by everything about him. As he gave the infertility lecture that day, my heart was pounding. After his lecture, I distinctly remember going to stand beside him. I was delighted to be enveloped in his energy field. Deep in my soul, I remembered him as if we had known each other forever.

I graduated from nursing school and received my credentials. I began to look for my first official position as a registered nurse. The same friend, the one who sat by me that day in class, called and announced, "That cute Dr. Scott has an opening for an office nurse." She still worked at his clinic. My heart skipped a beat, realizing the universe might be guiding me. I went the very next day to apply. My only thought was that I wanted to be near him.

I interviewed with the Director of Personnel. She was a very warm and special woman who would later become a devoted friend. She told me that Dr. Scott had specifically requested a nurse with experience. I convinced her that I was a passionate nurse, a quick study, and I hoped for an opportunity to prove it. I had good grades, hospital work experience, and outstanding recommendations. She agreed to set up an interview with the doctor.

The next day, looking my best in my favorite purple wool suit, I went to meet this mystery man face to face. He was soft spoken and very sweet. He asked me quite a few questions. Of them, he wanted to know if I minded working late hours. He also inquired how I felt about abortion, pre-marital sex, and other controversial subjects related to women's health care. Being single, late hours were fine. As far as pregnancy termination, I believed a woman had the right to choose. He explained to me that he offered many services to his patients, and some were controversial and difficult. I assured him that I was neutral on all the gynecology options offered women at the time.

Despite the fact that I was confident in the interview, being close to him I became very hot and flushed. I left full of hope and excitement. He called me that night to tell me I had the job. I told myself it would only be a temporary position, but I was ecstatic!

What good fortune had befallen me to be given the opportunity to work with this dedicated physician. Married men were definitely off limits, but I admit I was quite taken with him.

My career in women's health care was launched. I quickly realized that I would do anything to please my new boss. I was determined to enjoy the nursing position and to conceal my growing attraction. I learned extensively from him. He was a caring and compassionate advocate for women as well as an experienced surgeon. This doctor was a very intelligent man, passionate about his work, and eager to teach. We worked long rewarding hours together. To my knowledge, every woman in our practice respected and appreciated him. I discovered that many women have a special, trusting relationship with their gynecologist. As it turned out, his respect for females, as a gender, extended beyond the office. He once told me that he felt women were superior to men in many ways.

It became quite apparent, from the start, that the doctor was not in any hurry to leave the office at night. Building the practice was his priority. He told me not to turn away any patients and to double book them if necessary. We often worked long after the clinic was closed, seeing to every woman's needs. It was such a thrill to be a registered nurse at last. Dr. Scott was a humanitarian, first and foremost, and everything else in his life took a back seat to this. He helped found the first Planned Parenthood clinic in the community where he donated his services for years. I assisted him in this endeavor. He would rather catch babies than watch a football game.

I consciously continued to make plans to move on with my life, even though I was powerlessness over my blossoming love. Working so closely with him was only confusing me further. Eventually, I would realize he was experiencing the same feelings for me! I had no idea until one night after a clinic party and a few drinks, he kissed me.

From that day forward, we would fall into each other's arms at every opportunity. I quickly realized that my life would never be the same. This was not the way I had planned it. I never dreamt I would fall in love with a married man. The conflict I felt was enormous. Shame, delight, and fear all descended upon me at once. The chemistry between us was palpable. How could something so exciting and wonderful be so wrong? Timing is so important in life. Even though I was naive, vulnerable, and heavily influenced by my hormones and emotions, this was no excuse to violate my own sense of right and wrong.

We both did our best to deal with our attraction as we went about the day to day business of running a demanding practice. I would eventually discover that his personal life was unraveling long before I came into the picture. I am certain his feelings for me only made the marriage more difficult. We muddled through the complicated situation.

Ultimately, there was no denying our love or our burning desire to be together. I have many regrets from that early chapter but loving him was never a choice. Even though he was sixteen years my senior, I did not feel a large gap in our ages. He was youthful for his age, and I was quite mature for mine. The years of our affair were so unbelievably stressful. At the risk of sounding cliché; it seemed we truly were soulmates meeting up to write another chapter.

I am quite certain it quickly became clear to our colleagues how fond we were of each other. I was shocked at the intensity of his feelings for me. There is great power in the *forbidden*. I felt so alive. For months, we tried to convince each other that this was just a passing infatuation. We believed our secret would endure. Together, we also had the delusion that we could keep this aspect of our lives compartmentalized and separate from our work. I was inexperienced in affairs of the heart. I didn't want to live a deception. I certainly did not want to hurt anyone. I found myself secretly wanting him to work out his marriage so that I could be relieved of these conflicting and painful choices.

We came to realize that neither of us had the courage to walk away. I did not tell a soul of our liaison. We tried to convince ourselves otherwise, but true love cannot be hidden away. It is a light that naturally expands. I felt deep shame over the lie I was living. The truth was that my career and love life were enmeshed.

We decided to end the affair. He said he wanted to put his marriage back together for the benefit of all concerned. At that point, I attempted to make plans to move on. I soon realized this was not meant to be. He informed me that they were going to marriage counseling. It was not long thereafter, he told me they had reached a mutual decision to divorce.

Loved ones were hurt by our selfish inability to control our passion for one another. In the end, the truth prevailed. I knew right from wrong. If I could relive that chapter of my life, I would have waited for him to be free. Beginnings are so important. In reflection, I believe a solid foundation is best built on honesty.

As time passed, we outlived the stigma of the affair. Our community and families accepted our past transgressions and our love for each other. I grew and learned from my mistakes. I vowed to always encourage and support his relationship with his children. Eventually, I attempted to make amends to his first wife.

The practice flourished. He sent me to Southern California to attend a program to become a licensed nurse practitioner. With these new capabilities, I would be better able to assist him in our growing practice. James also believed it was the best life insurance policy he could buy for me. During the four months I was away, we decided to get married. His divorce had been final for a year.

We hired a registered nurse, Ann, to take my place assisting him in the office. Ann worked for him for almost ten years. She described Dr. Scott as having a genuine smile that complimented every step he took. He could often be seen sauntering down the clinic hallways with his white lab coat swishing around him as a trail of pipe smoke wafted behind. He was self-effacing and didn't display any of the arrogance we sometimes saw in surgeons. He taught her to *always listen* to the patient and *never pass judgement*. He was generous with his time and skills, never turning away a patient for any reason. The delivery room staff said that Dr. Scott added confidence, calm, and humor to every situation.

He flew to Los Angeles on Memorial Day weekend, and we drove to Las Vegas to officially tie the knot. It had been four long years since the day he entered that classroom. At last, I was free to follow my heart. Despite everything we would have to overcome, our relationship grew in maturity and joy. We experienced a deep and abiding love for each other.

Loving and forgiving myself had become my difficult but necessary lesson. I began to realize how critical the quality of integrity is to inner peace.

CHAPTER 4

Making Choices

The soul is wise and would not inhabit a body if it were not to come to term.

~Emmanuel's Book

Working in a multi-specialty clinic has some definite advantages with regard to your own medical needs. The employees have immediate and total access to laboratory, radiology, medications, and to physicians of many specialties. In our OB-GYN department, it was commonplace for a female employee to be treated by the physician she worked for. If you had a gynecological problem, you would be in the stirrups for an exam. I had total faith and trust in my husband's skill as a physician and surgeon. He was my doctor, as well as my boss, best friend, and husband. It sounds complicated. Actually, it was quite natural.

Sometime during the first year of our marriage, I found myself a week late for my period. My breasts were tender, and I was exhausted. We were using a diaphragm for birth control because I had developed severe migraines on oral contraceptives. Knowing the failure rate was higher with the diaphragm, I went to James immediately with these symptoms. He said, "We better do a pregnancy test." This was all that was said. My adrenaline levels were already climbing at the mere thought of what this might mean to us. My blood pressure must have skyrocketed when I saw the results of the test. Sure enough, I was pregnant. We had never entertained this possibility.

That night, we sat down to discuss the situation. The first thing he said to me was, "Let's get you an appointment in Seattle to have this pregnancy terminated." I almost fainted on the spot. How could this be happening? I had never imagined being married and having an abortion. Legalizing abortion gave women reproductive choices. Seemingly, he had decided the fate of this pregnancy without even considering how I might feel about it. I realized James worked every day with these situations. He had likely become desensitized. I was his *wife*. This was also *his* pregnancy.

I questioned him, "Why? After all, we *are* married. It is not a shame to have an unplanned pregnancy."

He could see that I was definitely not on board with the idea of a pregnancy termination. He asked me, "Do you want a baby now?" In all honesty I did not, and I told him so. My career as a nurse practitioner was just beginning. Our marriage was new. All four of his kids were living with us which was a tremendous handful. I was working long hours and tending to a large home. "Sherry, I honestly believe my first obligation is to my four children. With the divorce and all of the adjustments involved, I believe we owe our newly blended family every possible chance for success. Bringing a baby into the situation right now would be a stressor none of us need or want. We have the option of choosing another, better time for a baby. Please, just consider what I am saying."

As usual, I knew that he was operating out of pure logic. The romantic in me wanted to embrace the idea of a baby. I needed to believe that it would magically be a wonderful experience. I did, however, realize that what he was saying was true. The dedication required to take care of a baby would involve sacrifice that we weren't prepared to make at that time. The conflict for me was my belief that if you become pregnant while married, you make the most of the situation. Perception being everything, I was thrown into a moral dilemma.

The truth was, I had married a man who believed in planned pregnancies and a woman's right to choose. In this case, a couple's right to choose. I could see there was no solution to the problem that would make all of us happy. I believed if I fought him on this, it would drive a wedge between us. We had to sacrifice something in order to move on. It was going to be our pregnancy.

From menarche to menopause, women sought our support for unplanned and unwanted pregnancies. After compassionate counseling, the procedure was performed in the hospital under anesthesia. Some of the hospital staff refused to assist the doctor due to their moral objections. We treated every patient with dignity and respect during this confusing and difficult time.

This was my body, and I felt very territorial about my womb. I found myself feeling paralyzed by fear and shame. How could I let this happen? I believed that women had a responsibility to use reliable birth control. If contraception failed, to be aware, and seek help as early as possible.

I was being asked to make a sacrifice that defied my personal values. I felt devastated and truly sick about the entire situation. Mostly, I was in shock. Abortion is an unsettling solution to an impossible question. I knew if it were my decision alone, I would choose to have a baby. I would love the baby and never look back. I soon realized that any shame I felt was a direct result of my judgement.

I was torn between respecting my husband, putting our blended family first, and my own desire to allow my body to nourish this pregnancy. My love, for my husband and our future life together, won out. I agreed to the pregnancy termination on one condition and one condition only. James wanted to know what that was. "You have to perform the termination yourself. I refuse to let a stranger handle the procedure. I trust you, and you are my doctor. You will handle this, or it won't be done." He knew I meant every word of what I said. Perhaps I felt this would be retribution for feeling the situation was impossible and unfair. All I can say is that it seemed the only way I could quell my fear. He agreed to my request. He said that he would perform the surgical procedure the next day. We would wait until the rest of the staff had left the office. It would be our private matter.

I can honestly tell you I felt a sense of betrayal, at first, followed by relief. My knight in shining armor wasn't going to rescue me from my crises in some fairy tale way. We would handle it together with courage and dignity. I felt as if I were standing outside of my body observing someone else going through the entire next day. When the work day was complete, I set up the instruments required for this minor surgical procedure. I positioned myself on the exam table, and I put my feet in the stirrups. To say I felt vulnerable would be quite an understatement.

I said a prayer, *"God* please help me forgive myself." I talked to the spirit I knew must be hovering around me. I asked her to return when the time was right. I promised to be lovingly receptive the next time. I intuitively felt a feminine energy. James gave me a local anesthetic. In a few moments, it was all over. The procedure was physically painful but not intolerable. I just kept thinking of releasing, letting go, and trusting *God* with the rest.

My husband, today my physician, helped me sit up. He put his arms around me, and we both wept. It was a sweet, loving, and sad moment for us. I was deeply touched at his emotion. I felt relieved that my love did indeed share this sense of loss with me. He was such a tender and sweet soul. His presence was always calming.

Two days later, I still felt pregnant. We did another pregnancy test, and it was *positive*. I was devastated. I told him, "I won't go through this again." If you missed the pregnancy, which can happen with early terminations, then I will think it is meant to be. We waited another agonizing two days, and the symptoms subsided. A repeat test was negative. By then, I was emotionally wrung out. I grieved for my unfinished pregnancy for a long time.

We moved forward with our life. I had an intrauterine device (IUD) inserted for better pregnancy protection. I asked *God* to send me some guidance regarding this very difficult decision. My compassion for women with unplanned and unwanted pregnancies was much deeper from that time forward. Once again, I was reminded of the importance of humility, and my heart cautioned me about judgement.

I never judged the decisions of our patients and always respected their right to choose. I was aware of the complexities I knew were inherent in each situation. It was time to give that gift to myself. Even though most patients were single adults, there were many times that a distraught woman came to us for pregnancy termination for herself or her teenage daughter. Some of these women were the same ones who fought the hardest against legalizing abortion. They marched with signs in front of our clinic. We never know how we will choose when life takes a different path than we had envisioned.

Many months later, when my emotions were back in balance, I was given this guidance dream: *I was caring for several little creatures. They were half human and half animal. They looked something like a seahorse (obviously representing fetuses). I dearly loved these little creatures. Without warning, they all died. We didn't kill them. They just spontaneously died. I was totally devastated by this loss. I felt deep sorrow and was beside myself with grief. In my inconsolable state, I thought that because they had died that I should give up my life as well. I injected a poison into my vein and lay down to die. I could actually feel my life force leaving my physical body. I suddenly became aware of all the little creatures coming back to life. They were just fine. I panicked, realizing that I was sacrificing my own life unnecessarily. Suddenly, James was at my side and extremely upset at my condition. I was very near death and extremely weak. I somehow managed to murmur to him what I had done, and which poison I had taken. He quickly found the antidote and injected it into me. I slowly came back to my full awake and healthy state. I was extremely grateful to be alive. At this point, a guiding voice said,* **"Destruction for the sake of creation is accepted. All of life is eternal."**

As I came out of the dream, I knew that this was *God's* reply to my question. It was a poignant lesson in always examining motives before making important decisions in life. Loving and forgiving myself were again my lessons.

CHAPTER 5

Enjoying the Ride

***And think not you can direct the course of love, for
love, if it finds you worthy, directs your course.***

~The Prophet

From this point forward, our love flourished.
We were a solid working team, and we served a very
large patient population. I was now a licensed nurse
practitioner and had built a practice of my own. I cared
for the non-surgical, uncomplicated cases, and James
cared for the rest. We continued to work long and very
hard hours every day. Our personal and professional
relationship was always extremely harmonious. We
were both very even tempered. There was a mutual
shared passion for women and their medical and
emotional needs.

There was one glitch. Early in our time together,
James told me that he didn't think he would ever be
truly happy. He felt a dark cloud in his life. I assumed
this was based on some of the choices he had made.
This news was devastating to a woman in love. I tried
to push the thought of his general malaise out of my
mind. I hoped he was grieving and that it would pass.
One morning, as he was having breakfast with me, he
smiled that warm beautiful smile of his. He took me by

the hand and he said, "Sweetheart, I just want you to know that I am extremely happy." It was a high point in our early married life. I knew we were going to be fine.

I gained confidence and trust in our future. His children were growing up and seemed to be adjusting. We made plans to have a child together. James wanted me to have a little girl to love. This would be his gift of love to me. He said I had given so much for him, and he wanted my life to feel complete. Our daughter was born five years into our marriage. Alysia was conceived on James' birthday. She was perfect in every way. The labor and delivery went as I had hoped, with my husband delivering our baby girl. Without a doubt, this was the happiest day of my life.

He looked at her and said, "She is feisty. I know she is a survivor." Little did we know that she would need those skills within a few short years. I loved her with the same passion I had for him. She became the focus of my life. I took six months off work before returning to my practice part time. I took parenting very seriously and would stop at nothing to give my baby every opportunity to be stimulated and happy.

By the time she was two, her precociousness was quite amazing. My dedication was evidenced in her evolution. She was very strong willed, funny, and engaging. She had a voracious appetite for books. I read to her for hours every day. This child was a born leader. I now had more time to develop friendships with other women who had small children. James and I had never been happier. He was more taken with this wee tot than he imagined possible. She captivated both of us with her immense spirit.

I began to develop more of my own interests. I loved psychology and holistic medicine. I was also keenly interested in metaphysics and spirituality. A good friend, Catrina, invited me to attend a class at the local community college. The course was on dreaming. The information was powerful for me. I had been aware of my dreams since childhood, and I was curious to know more on the subject. The professor was very knowledgeable. We conducted experiments with our dreams as well as keeping dream journals. We learned all the different types of dreams. Communication with the living or the dead, guidance, premonition and warning, problem solving, nonsense dreams were explained. We even discovered that we can dream for each other. I asked if I dreamed in color? That night I had a vivid dream of a color wheel! This would become an extremely useful tool on my spiritual journey.

To have a conscious connection with my *Higher Self* was intriguing. Once I began to pay closer attention to my dreams, they became more significant and applicable to my daily and spiritual life. My *Higher Self* began to send timely, significant coded messages to help prepare me for loss.

I began to notice more coincidences taking place in my life. I could see a deeper meaning to many of the events as they unfolded. I realized that I sometimes telepathically shared thoughts with others. James and I often communicated in this way. I developed an interest in an afterlife and wondered if any proof of one existed. I read books on death, grief, and stories that expanded my thinking regarding these topics.

I was also finding my own autonomy as a woman. I began feeling a sense of power that I had not known. My thirst for spiritual meaning brought a new energy and interest in my life. I was very moved by *Man's Search for Meaning,* by Victor Frankl. The horror of the holocaust is a powerful study in human nature. The idea of *learned optimism,* as a tool for dealing with devastating loss, was intriguing to me. It helped me gain perspective on my potential for resiliency in the face of adversity.

Around this time, a young doctor in our clinic became gravely ill with terminal cancer. We were extremely upset by the situation. He had several small children and a thriving medical practice. It seemed that love was all that mattered as his life came to a close. I was very fond of this man. When it became clear he had turned the last corner, we were told that we had little time left to say our goodbyes. I felt overwhelmingly compelled to see him. I mustered up the courage to look him in the eyes and tell him I loved him as a physician and as a human being.

I found the experience emotional, sad, and exhilarating all at the same time. I was shocked at the fortitude it took to face his death. I understood it was a sacred experience to be at a dying person's bedside. I instinctively realized there was much to be learned from those at the edge of this life.

I was not able to attend his funeral, but James did. I had said my farewell. He was agitated regarding the event. He said, "Don't ever do that to me! Never have a sad funeral with organ music and all that heaviness. Celebrate my life. Please don't mourn my passing." I promised him I would do my best when the time came.

Death continued to be on his mind. A few weeks later, he came home with a medical journal he had been reading. He said, "Please read this poem about death. This is how I hope it is. I want this read at my memorial service." It was the following Indian poem:

Do not stand by my grave and weep
I am not there. I do not sleep.
I am a thousand winds that blow.
I am the diamond glint on snow.
I am the sunlight on ripened grain.
I am the gentle autumn rain.
When you wake in the morning hush
I am the swift, uplifting rush
Of quiet birds in circling flight
I am the soft starlight at night
Do not stand at my grave and cry
I am not there. I did not die.
~Unknown

Wow! It was so out of character for him to share at this level. I read it and was touched by the beautiful imagery of the continuation of life beyond death. I said to him, "Well Sweetie, you better carry it in your wallet because how would I ever know where to find it when you die?" We both laughed about this fact, and no more was said. It was a strange conversation to be having with my seemingly vibrant husband.

A few months later, one of his sons graduated from university. We sat on the opposite side of the room from his first wife. I thought how sad it was that even at this important event they didn't acknowledge each other. It seemed an unnecessary loss for the entire family. It had been many years with still no resolution to the past.

James was incredibly proud of his kids. He always gave credit to his former wife for their children's accomplishments. After the ceremony, I felt a surge of anxiety that I get right before I do something courageous. I walked up to her and said, "Congratulations, you must be very proud. I commend you on your parenting success." She was taken back by my boldness but thanked me, nonetheless. I realized that I couldn't change past decisions, but I could do something about my choices today. I was living up to the vow I had made to myself ... to do what I believed was right.

A week later, I received a letter from her. She thanked me for approaching her. I was so surprised that the risk I had taken had been received as it was intended. I called my good friend, Lynn, to share the story. I said, "Someday we will have to attend a birth, or a wedding, and it is time to heal the past. This is a start."

My friend said, "It could be a funeral. You never know." I would soon look back in awe at those prophetic words.

Around the same time, I read a book that had a story in it about a couple who had agreed to give one another a sign of life after death. Two days after the first mate died, the surviving spouse went out the back door and discovered that a bush her husband had given her for an anniversary present was in full bloom. It had never bloomed in all the years since the gift was given. She felt strongly that this was a message from him.

I shared the story with James. "Could we have that same pact? Would you do that for me? It would be the last thing you could give me. If I could know there was an afterlife and that you were okay, it would mean so much." He promised solemnly that he would honor my request if it was possible, and if there was indeed life after death. He was historically quite the skeptic on the topic. I said, "Make it obvious so I don't miss it!"

The really strange thing about this conversation was that James was very logical and scientifically oriented. He had never been interested in spiritual or metaphysical matters, always shying away from any discussions regarding these topics. He once told me,

"It's a nice thought that there is an afterlife, but I'm too busy living here and now to be bothered with the idea." His sudden willingness to touch on the subject implied a major shift in his thinking. I understandably regarded it as the natural aftermath to our friend's recent death.

I could feel myself becoming very aware of a change in my own perception of life around me. I began to sense that I was watching life unfold as well as living that same life. It was a natural feeling of detachment. I decided to listen more carefully to my inner voice. I felt a strong nudge to read more on death. I read books by Elizabeth Kubler-Ross. Her writing impacted me greatly. She was a pioneer of her time. I pondered death and loss. As I now look back, I realize this was a tremendous level of kismet. It was if a super-natural force was guiding me to prepare for loss.

A couple of weeks later, we went sailing on Lake Washington. It was a crisp day in June. I remember it as a special day. Our little girl was with us. I can still recall her vivid yellow life jacket, and how nimble she was exploring the sailboat with her oldest brother.

James loved to take photographs and considered himself an amateur photography buff. He was always taking pictures of all of us. I took the camera out of his hands and said, "Let me take a picture of you. If you weren't here we would want some pictures of you." As I focused on the scene, he gazed at me with a loving look reserved only for me. Alysia was tucked safely by his side sucking her favorite two fingers. It was one of those special warm and fuzzy moments forever framed in my mind and heart. The developed photos of that day would arrive two weeks later. It felt like a gift from *God,* and I was moved beyond words.

CHAPTER 6

A Light Goes Out

Live as though it were your last day on earth. Some day you will be right.

~Robert Anthony

My husband and I once attended a workshop for physicians and their wives. The speaker was a well-respected psychiatrist. He drew a pie shaped chart and filled it in with various aspects of life. For example; marriage, family, work, recreation, spirituality, health and hobbies. He stressed the importance of balance. The specialist emphasized one point that I have never forgotten. He said he could predict how a person would live and die and even approximately when. He believed this was based on one factor. This predictor was how we handle loss in our life. All losses, big and small, are important. I remember getting a psychic rush and looking at James. I knew in my heart that he had not and did not handle loss well. His way of coping was to bury his emotions. He had not taken good care of himself. He smoked, got little sleep, and his eating habits were marginally healthy. He always put his patients before his personal needs.

We had been married for seven years. As spring turned to summer, I made a mental note of a change in

James' aerobic stamina. He became winded easily. I was constantly reminding him to get more rest. Those long sleepless nights spent delivering babies seemed to be taking quite a toll on him. This particular week, he came home every night and took his bike out for a strenuous ride. He went alone. I had never seen him do this. I would later find out he was testing his cardiovascular strength. I also noticed a dusky appearance to his skin. He was only forty-six, yet there were days when he seemed much older.

On Thursday, he picked roses from the garden and brought them to me. He said, *"Please don't ever say I never brought you flowers."* I looked at his rugged face drawn from the lack of sleep. I hugged him and replied, "Okay Sweetie, I won't." I carefully put them in my favorite vase. I had a prickly rush all over my body at this unusual statement. Those would be the last flowers he would ever pick for me. Less than twenty-four hours later, his words seemed dramatically significant. My love and best friend would be gone from this life forever. Did he instinctively know he was preparing to leave?

On Friday, James went into the cardiology department of our clinic and put himself on the treadmill. One of the cardiology nurses found him there. She insisted a cardiologist evaluate him. Apparently, he was experiencing a heaviness in his chest along with radiating pain down his left arm. These are all classic symptoms of heart problems. The treadmill electrocardiogram results were normal. Because of his symptoms, the cardiologist insisted he be scheduled for further testing on Monday.

Monday never came for James. When he told me about the symptoms and the upcoming tests, he added, "I may be following in my mother's footsteps." I knew that his mother had died from coronary failure at the age of fifty-two. I was unable to say anything. Paralyzed at this thought, I was again aware of a strange sensation of hyper-awareness coming over me. This time it was a feeling of *impending doom*.

Saturday was the fourth of July. We had plans to go camping with a group of our friends, and I was excited. I looked forward to getting away. He delivered several babies during the night. The lack of sleep left him a little cranky that morning. I remember an inner voice saying, as we left the house, "What if this were the last day you ever spend with him? Would you want to spend any of it bickering over minor things?" I just hopped in the pick-up, put on a happy face, strapped our toddler into her car seat, and away we went.

As we took the scenic drive up the highway, an interesting conversation took place. He began telling me how much he had loved watching me mother our child. He also told me that I was the best nurse he had ever worked with. He said this was because I intently listened to the patients. Once again, it was unusual for him to verbalize his sentiments. I thanked him for sharing his feelings. We went on to talk about our life together. We often took the time to express our gratitude for our love and the life we were living. This intimate life review was definitely a first.

The remainder of the day was spent in fellowship with several other couples and their children. Our good friends and neighbors, Teresa and Larry, came with their family. She brought brownies which was James' favorite desert. I confided to her that day, "I could be a young widow. James is having heart symptoms." She said, "Oh my gosh, don't think that way!" I did think it, but I certainly didn't believe it. It was a strange day in many ways. I felt like everything was happening in slow motion. This made me acutely aware of the smallest of details.

I commented to Lynn, "James looks radiant today, hardly like someone with a heart problem." It seemed like his energy field was more alive, and even his color had improved. In the afternoon, he rafted the river with the guys.

When he returned, he took a nap with his little girl. This was another first. After our traditional BBQ that evening, we had fireworks around the campfire. Some of the couples drove home. About twelve of us were going to stay the night. One of the kids got a spark in his eye, from the fireworks, and he was screaming for help. James rushed him into the cabin and rinsed his eye out with water, after which he was fine. We all had our adrenaline pumping though! Shortly after the excitement, Alysia fell asleep in her daddy's arms by the campfire. He tenderly put her to bed. She typically was a real Momma's baby. The extra affection they were expressing for each other all day was touching and notable to me.

We all snuggled around the fire, star gazing, as was our usual ritual at our river property. James then quietly left the group and went into the trailer telling me as he left, "I'm going to get a glass of milk … I have heartburn." After a few minutes, I began to get anxious and I went in to check on him. I know that heartburn is a classic symptom of a heart attack. I found him on his knees clutching his chest. He was swearing and saying, "It hurts so much, this is *horrible*, damn it, damn it!"

I flung open the door and yelled out to the group, "Does anyone know CPR? I think James is having a heart attack!"

The men in the circle sprang into action. One of the guys was a fireman. He shouted out, "*I do!*"

I said a silent, "Thank you, *God.*"

He was in so much pain that he was unable to stand up. The guys picked him up and carried him to the only car there, a Ford Pinto. The rest of us had brought pick-ups. I remember grabbing a pack of cigarettes and stuffing them in my blue sweatshirt pocket thinking, "I'm going to need these." I asked our close friend, Dick, to drive. I knew the two-lane winding road to the nearest town (thirty-five miles) would likely be populated with drinking party goers. I yelled out for someone to go to a phone booth and notify the hospital that we were coming. This was before the days of cell phones. Alysia was still sleeping. Lynn assured me she would stay with her. My only thought, at this point, was the safety of all of us. It was late, eleven-thirty on the fourth of July.

I asked the fireman, whose name was Bruce, to ride in the back seat. I did not want to be the one giving my husband mouth to mouth resuscitation if it came to that. I was shaking uncontrollably. As we left for the hospital, James sat up and was perfectly coherent for a few moments. He said, "I feel better." I had a surge of relief pass through me.

This was immediately followed by another episode of *crushing* chest pain. He was forced to lie down with his head in Bruce's lap. I took his hand in mine and monitored his irregular pulse. All the while, I was reassuring him that he would be alright. My adrenaline levels were extremely high at this point. In fact, I thought I would explode. I kept telling Dick to be careful. We had all had a few drinks celebrating the holiday, obviously never thinking we would be on the road so late. This most certainly would have been a good night for a designated driver.

James squeezed my hand twice. It was that loving reassuring squeeze he had given me countless times before. Then his pulse stopped. He began this labored, noisy, guttural, diaphragmatic breathing as if each breath took every muscle in his chest. I would later discover that sometimes after death the lungs continue to attempt to breathe. I knew he had left me after he squeezed my hand. I jumped in the back seat (thank the Lord I am a small woman). I wedged myself between the back of the passenger seat and the bench seat he was stretched out on. "*Breathe*, damn it, *breathe*, *breathe*, damn it, *breathe!*" I just kept shouting at him and begging him to keep breathing. I didn't know what else to do at that point. After a few moments, his respirations ceased. Bruce started giving him mouth to mouth resuscitation, and I began chest compressions.

We worked on him for the twenty more long minutes it took Dick to negotiate the drive to the nearest hospital. Gratefully, in spite of the circumstances, he got us there safely. All I could think was, "What comes next? What will I do? What will I say to them? It's been too long … too long without a heartbeat … too long without oxygen." The emergency staff ran out with a stretcher, and they managed to get him out of the car. They immediately took over the CPR. I felt so relieved and grateful for the help. Amazingly, his pupils were still reactive. This meant we had managed a satisfactory attempt at getting oxygen to his brain.

Much of what happened next is a blur. I knew I needed to call our cardiologist friend for advice. Someone got the phone number for me. He answered right away, and I began sobbing. He told me he couldn't understand me, and I must stop crying. I managed to do the impossible. I stifled my sobs. I told him James was at the Arlington hospital having a coronary. We had been resuscitating him for twenty minutes. He said he would be right there. It took another forty minutes for him to arrive.

Meanwhile, I kept going to the doorway of the room they had put him in. I observed their frantic efforts to shock him in an attempt to get his heart started. There was no response. Watching his body jump with each electrical discharge, I was forced to accept the futility of the effort. When the cardiologist arrived, I was tremendously grateful to see a familiar face, one I trusted implicitly.

He assessed the situation and then asked to speak to me privately. "Sherry, we have two options at this point. We can take James to Seattle (sixty-five miles away), open him up and do a bypass surgery. This is to try to get his heart restarted. The other option is to stop the CPR and pronounce death right now. He has been down for over an hour. What do you want to do?"

"What do I want to do? I can't make that decision!" I felt like someone else was talking. My voice sounded so far away.

He said, "You *must* decide."

I asked, "What would you do if it were your wife?"

"He said, "I can't answer that question. You must decide now … There is no time to waste." I took a deep breath and tried to calm myself.

I thought about the right thing to do. "James, what do you want me to do?" I hoped he was somehow able to communicate with me. I was certain, he was hovering and observing the situation.

Suddenly, it came to me. James believed in quality of life. He did not believe in saving babies who were likely to be affected neurologically. He would not want me to save him for a probable life on a respirator or severely brain damaged. "Stop the resuscitation." Those were the hardest three words I have ever said. My heart sank. It was so final. I felt like I caved in on myself at that moment. My lover, my best friend, the father of my child, he meant so many things to me.

The order was given. All resuscitation efforts were stopped, and death was pronounced. I asked the medical team to please leave the room. I wanted to be with him while his body was still warm. I draped myself over his chest and embraced him one last time. I sobbed hysterically until I had nothing left to express. I reluctantly left the room and joined the others. We hugged and gave each other words of comfort and appreciation. Everyone had given all they could to save his life.

It wasn't meant to be. He was forty-six years old. Myocardial infarctions which occur under the age of fifty are usually fatal. The heart has not had time to develop a collateral blood supply to help the oxygen starved heart if a clot occludes a main artery. They asked if I wanted an autopsy. I questioned if there would be any benefit to his family to have one done? The cardiologist felt certain that he had severe coronary artery disease with a genetic predisposition. I said no to the autopsy.

I had to choose a funeral home to send his body to and tell them whether I wanted burial or cremation. Interestingly, James had told me a few months before that he did not want to be cremated. So many decisions to make at a time when you want to just go crawl in a hole somewhere. I thought, "These are things all couples should discuss ahead of time." They gave me his wallet, eye glasses, and watch. Holding his personal effects, the reality of my sweetheart's death began to sink in.

In spite of the shock, all I could think about was Alysia. How would I tell her? She was only two and a half, and the thought was devastating. I told Dick and Bruce to go back to our camping spot and be with their families. I knew that Lynn would take good care of Alysia. It was decided that the cardiologist would drive me home. I am certain I was in shock at this point. As you can imagine, I had already smoked a few of those cigarettes. At that point in time, smoking was allowed in hospital waiting rooms. Strange as it seems today, many of the doctors and nurses smoked.

I felt like I was the heroine of some melodrama. The curtain had just gone up for the big performance. I think we humans should be required to take some sort of training in appropriateness for when life takes such a dramatic turn. People say the silliest things when they are put on the spot. Our friendly cardiologist was no exception. On the drive home he asked, "I guess this means you won't be having the clinic picnic at your house next week?"

I thought, "If only he knew how ridiculous that sounds to me right now." It was, however, comedic relief. I can easily imagine how awkward and stressful that drive was for him.

He walked me into our empty house. I assured him I would be fine. Immediately, I was consumed by emotional pain I had never imagined possible. I rushed up to our bedroom and flung open his closet. I buried my face in his clothes hoping to capture his scent. I wanted to feel his energy in any way that I could. I felt indescribably empty inside. I cried and cried for what seemed like a very long time before I managed to calm myself. I began to face the responsibility that came with being the doctor's wife and now widow. I remembered the *one day at a time* teaching for living with life's challenges. I thought, "Right now it is five minutes at a time for me." Staying in the present moment was the only tool that could give me sanity. If my mind began to wander to the future, a future without him, I thought I would break in two. I was alone with my shattered emptiness.

Who do you inform first? This man had so many loved ones in his life. I decided the right thing to do was to call his first wife, the mother of his children. I had many times made the wrong decisions where she was concerned. I was going to show her every respect possible. I thought that she would want to be the one to tell her children of their father's sudden death. It was the middle of the night by now. She sleepily answered the phone, and my heart skipped a beat. My voice was cracking and shaking with grief. She was at first disoriented about who was calling. I had to identify myself again. "James died tonight. He had a heart attack and they couldn't save him."

"I wanted you to be the first to know. You shared more of his life than I did. I know you will want to be the one to give the news to your children." She was understandably shocked and agreed to carry the devastating news to their four adult kids. She thanked me for including her. I felt good about this decision, even though my heart ached at the thought of how much pain this loss would cause each of them. Who should I notify next?

I called my husband's father who resided in Kentucky at the time. I have never heard such a primal scream from a human being as I did when I gave him the news. We cried together on the phone that night. This was the second son he had lost, the first one dying from ulcerative colitis in his twenties. It is so unnatural to lose a child at any age. I sobbed, "I am so sorry, I am just so sorry." I didn't know what else to say. I felt such compassion for him.

I then called my family and his family. I called, and I called until I couldn't think of anyone else. Each time I told the story, it became more real to me. As family came that night, we did our best to comfort each other. Energetically, my heart was bleeding. How would I ever heal?

I really needed some rest. I cried myself to sleep that night. The emptiness of our bed haunted me. I thought of all the women who had lost their mates, and I cried for them as well. I thanked *God* that I had the resources, skills, and most importantly- love in my life to get through this.

That morning at six, I had a lucid dream: ***I dreamt that James didn't die. He was at my side the entire time. Nobody could see him but me.*** It turned out to be a very prophetic dream.

CHAPTER 7

A Child's Sorrow

Your life unfolds in proportion to your courage.

~Danielle La Porte

Upon rising the next morning, I was exhausted from all my crying throughout the night. There was a strange quietness in the house. I felt drained, empty, and alone. The void was almost unbearable. I was immediately aware of a clear voice inside my head urging me to get up and face the day and to embrace all that was possible. This was my story, and today was the first day of a new chapter. Following this thought, a rush of anger flooded through me ... totally raw emotion. I had read about anger being a normal part of grieving. Knowing it was important not to push it away, I fully accepted it. I used the impetus of that emotion to shower and dress. What does a grieving widow wear on her first day? I settled on my usual, favorite, comfortable outfit of jeans and a t-shirt.

It was seven in the morning. The only thought I had was, "I desperately need to be with my friend Teresa." She lived two houses down the street. I knew she would do anything for me. When she picked up the phone, I said, "Teresa, James died last night. He had a heart attack, and we tried everything to save him with no success."

She gasped, "Oh my *God*, no! I'll be right down." She walked in the door, threw her arms around me and said, "What can I do?" We hugged and cried together.

"I need some cigarettes. I know it sounds awful, but this is no time to give up my crutches." In that moment, this seemed like something I could actually control.

She compassionately said, "Of course, let's go." We went to the little mini-market around the block, and I bought several packs. I remember sitting in the car outside of the market. I told her everything that had taken place since the previous afternoon.

We were both amazed at the fact that I had shared, "I could be a widow." I really didn't believe it when I said it. How could I have known?

She made it quite clear that she would do anything in her power to help me get through this ordeal. I felt so loved and had such gratitude. My life was blessed with many loving friends and a supportive family. I felt incredibly safe that morning. She was my true earth angel. I knew deep inside that I would survive. I sent her home and told her I would be in touch.

At this point, I could start making more phone calls, but all I wanted to do was be with my love. I missed him so much. My heart ached with a searing physical pain in my chest. It was as if someone had taken out my heart, ripped it in two and shoved it back into the empty cavity. How would my heart ever recover from this assault? My world was destroyed. I prayed,

"*God* please help me." The answer I received was to believe in my own strength. I felt assisted and guided. I knew I was living out the destiny I had, at some level, agreed to. I come from a long line of strong women. Their role modeling echoed in my whole being.

I had notified the intimate members of our joint families. I knew my precious baby girl would be brought to me soon. What would I say to her? She was so young. Would she understand? I was consumed by my anxiety, yet a growing sense of purpose and courage began to surface within me.

I realized, in that moment, that I was the only person who could properly attend to the many details and emotional issues that must be handled. I needed and wanted to be the one to set the stage. Alysia was quite precocious, but this was such an enormous loss for a small child in her formative years. I felt physically ill at the thought of what this parental abandonment could do to my baby's emotional development.

I heard the car pull up. I went outside to retrieve her from the car seat. Dick had driven her. He said she woke up in the middle of the night, never asked a question about where her parents were but just looked around. Alysia had been totally silent ever since. There she sat, looking quite pensive and sucking on those two favorite fingers of her right hand. I remember thinking it was a blessing she had some habits to comfort herself with. She was going to need them. I was shaking all over knowing I had to break the news to her now.

I took my sweet little girl in the house. She looked around obviously realizing something was very wrong. Her adorable bubbly personality had gone underground. It seemed replaced by a serious and sullen demeanor. I carried her over to the plaid loveseat in our family room. I then sat down with her on my lap facing me.

I will never forget a word of the exact conversation this Mommy and her little two-year-old had about her Daddy's death: "Alysia, Mommy has something very sad to tell you." I choked back the sobs that were so close to the surface.

My baby asked, "What, Mommy?"

"Last night, after Daddy put you to bed he began to have pains in his chest. We took him to the hospital, and the doctors tried to make him better. Unfortunately, they couldn't. Daddy couldn't stay in his body anymore because his body was so sick, and he died. Daddy doesn't live in his body anymore. We won't ever see him again. He has gone to live in a new body in Heaven with *God*." She started to cry, and then I started to cry. We sat there holding each other and sobbing for several minutes. The powerlessness and empathy I felt for both of us was gut-wrenching.

Next, a truly remarkable thing happened. This incredible little child choked back her sobs and said to me, "Mommy, I just want to ask you one thing."

I said, "What's that, Honey?"

She went on, "Mommy, are you going to be okay?"

I said, "Yes, I will be okay, Honey."

She looked me straight in the eyes and said, "Then I will be okay too, Mommy." With that, she got off my lap and went into James' office where she stayed for about fifteen minutes. She quietly sat in the space they had so often shared. When she came out, there were no more tears, yet a deep sadness hovered around her.

I again reassured her, "Even though we will miss Daddy and there will be more tears, we will someday be happy again." Then I told her, "Daddy's body is still here even though he doesn't live in it. You can say good-bye to his body tomorrow if you want to." I explained to her about funeral homes, caskets, and cemeteries.

She sweetly said, "I do want to, Mommy."

"After that, they will bury his body in the ground." I did my best to explain these things in a gentle yet matter of fact manner.

Now all of this may seem like a lot to expect a toddler to understand. Miraculously, I had been reading a children's book to Alysia about these grandmas who die and what dying means. We had actually talked about death and that it meant you wouldn't be here anymore. She was two and half and no doubt an old soul. Her capacity for understanding continually amazed me. I had done some reading on discussing death with children and was probably better equipped to deal with this than anyone I knew at the time.

Deciding this was enough heaviness for one morning, I took Alysia down to Teresa's to play with her best friend, Johnny. The funeral home had called and asked me to bring clothing for James' body. They said they were ready. This is where all that funeral training with my grandmother started becoming quite useful. I thought about the fact that yesterday we were roasting wieners over a campfire, laughing, loving, and enjoying the summer. Today, I was choosing my lover's clothing for burial. How bizarre is life? I went to his closet and mused at how the bodies in caskets I had seen in the past were all dressed up in their Sunday outfits.

I thought about my James and how he had special favorite clothes that were comfortable to him. One example, being that silly fluorescent red t-shirt trimmed in purple. He put it on every day when he came home from work. I tried to give it away once, and he got quite upset with me. We had laughed about his attachment to it. I saved that smelly shirt for months to get a whiff of him.

I settled on his favorite, brown flannel sport coat, along with a yellow shirt and tie. Attending to these details seemed the critically important last personal duties of a wife. There were more tears and reminiscing over his clothing as I remembered him in every article hanging in his closet. I knew I wouldn't keep his personal effects for long. It was just too painful. Later that week, I let family members take what they wanted.

I could feel the anger rising up in me once again. Off I went to find the funeral home. I had never been there but had driven by in the past. I walked into the director's office and began this conversation: "My name is Sherry Scott. These are my husband's clothes which you requested. I want to see his body."

He rose, shook my hand and said, "Mrs. Scott, it is not customary to view the body before it is clothed and placed in a casket. You must pick out a casket first. Then come back tomorrow after we have everything in order."

I know this made perfect sense, but I was a woman possessed by the desire to be with her man even if he was dead! "He is my husband. I have seen him naked plenty of times, and I want to see him *now!*" I must have said it in such a forceful and serious way that the poor fellow didn't dare refuse me. He kindly showed me out of his office to a stairway. He told me to follow the stairs down to the door on the left directly across from the casket room. I marched down those stairs just like I knew what I was doing.

I flung open the door to the embalming room, and there lay his body. I was enraged at this point. There was a sterile white sheet pulled up under his chin. I threw the sheet back, exposing him in his lovely birthday suit. "James, how could you do this to me? How could you just drop dead? How could you leave Alysia without a daddy? How could you abandon me without even saying goodbye? I am so pissed at you right now, if you weren't already dead I swear I'd kill you myself." I made myself laugh with that last threat. I had a good cry and then I began to realize just how weird this all was.

I looked around the stark white, *very cold,* embalming room. It resembled a small surgical suite. The instruments were all neatly laid out on a tray next to the slab table. The smell of death is not at all pleasant especially mixed with the preservatives which had been pumped into his body. I could see the bruising from the attempted resuscitation. I relived the entire emergency room scene from the previous night. I ran my hands all over his body, tenderly remembering the physical aspect of our relationship. I held his hands in mine. How I loved those gentle hands. The hands that had ushered so many little lives into this world. I remembered his compassionate spirit and his loving touch. I said good-bye to our physical life together. I had a feeling he was in the room with me, and I talked with him about his life and his death. I told him I would make certain all the details were attended to properly.

I thanked him for our life. I went from rage to gratitude for the miracle of love. I felt so incredibly fulfilled, understanding why we had taken the risks to be together, and now knowing how short our time was to be. I stayed with his naked body until I felt at peace with his departure. I was grateful that he did not have to suffer very much. If it was his time to leave this earth, he left at the peak of his career. He had much love and respect in his life. I felt no more shock, denial, or anger, just sadness and peace. I covered him and went into the casket room.

Another surreal experience awaited me. The casket room was also *very cold*. Don't they ever turn on the heat in these places? The caskets were propped open to show their satin interiors. By now, the director had joined me again. I thanked him for indulging my request to see James' body. He tried to steer me to some lovely, very expensive pieces. I spotted a beautiful oak casket in the corner. It was the only wooden box in the room, and it was also the least expensive. James was frugal to a fault. Nothing excited him more than a Blue Light Special at K-Mart! I could feel him urging me to be practical. He also liked wood, making this an easy decision. I said, "Give me this one," as I pointed to the beautiful oak casket.

I went upstairs, signed the papers, and discussed the remainder of the arrangements. The director started asking me questions about his past, his life, and about his burial and funeral arrangements. It is just so much to have to deal with. He told me I would need to bring in his discharge papers from the Air Force in order to get his veteran's benefits. I could hardly fathom that yesterday we were planning our next vacation.

I somehow made the necessary decisions. I decided on a memorial service, and I wanted only close family members and friends to be allowed to view his body. There would be a cemetery plot purchased in

Port Townsend where he had fond boyhood memories. The cemetery overlooked Puget Sound. Even in our disbelief, the family managed to get through the final arrangements.

This is only day one without my love. I have just begun this widow's duties associated with my husband's death. My head felt like it was stuffed with cotton, and I was fighting a consuming sadness every minute. My spirit felt like it had been catapulted out of my body. Even though I'm certain I was still in shock, I knew I was in total control of the current situation. This sense of purpose was some comfort for me.

CHAPTER 8

The Visitation

And when the earth shall claim your limbs, then shall you truly dance.

~The Prophet

It was day two since my life went upside down. The word was out, and the phone was ringing off the hook. I wanted to answer every call. It was important to me not to miss one minute of what was transpiring during this first week. I knew I needed the distractions and moral support that life would send my way. The casseroles and potted plants began to arrive. The parade of visitors, all with their sincerity and condolences, kept me occupied. James was so loved by the entire community. Our medical practice was quite large. I mused at how these patients would manage to find medical care in his absence. We would never turn anyone away often at the expense of our own rest and personal life. It seemed in many ways senseless now, yet this was his legacy. My immediate family was devastated and at a loss as to how to be of any real support. They also lived two states away.

As far as the traditional casseroles, we do need to eat even when it seems like the world should stop. I certainly had no appetite, but family and friends found eating a necessary distraction. The best part about getting all the casseroles is that it gives you purpose and human contact when you really need it. Returning the dishes is also a gift. If you feel compelled to cook for the grieving, I encourage you to do so.

The funeral home called. "Your husband is ready for viewing."

"You mean my husband's *body?*" I corrected him. It seemed critical to separate *him* from his remains in order to keep reminding myself that he no longer resided in the flesh.

He stammered, "Yes, yes of course, his body." I thanked him.

I took Alysia aside and after a big deep breath, I said, "We can go say good-bye to Daddy's body today. It is in a box and it looks like he is sleeping, but he isn't. He died, and he doesn't live in that body any more. He lives in Heaven now. He can see us, but we can't see him. We get one last chance to see his body. After that, it will be buried in the ground. Mommy is going to go see it. Would you like to go with me? We can stop at McDonald's for lunch on the way if you want." (This was her favorite activity.) I purposely tried to make it all sound just as normal as anything else we might do that day.

She was resolute, "Yes, Mommy. I want to go."

With a great deal of trepidation, off we went. Some of my friends were horrified that I would take such a small child to view his body. I had studied the subject of children and death. I knew it was a choice she could make even at her young age. It would help her to see that he couldn't come home and also give her a chance to start letting go. Accepting the certainty of his death was hard enough for the adults. Imagine a child who had last been left by her Daddy tucking her into bed. We stopped at McDonald's for lunch. My heart was pounding the entire time. Not knowing exactly how this was going to turn out yet having her welfare first and foremost in my mind, I summoned the courage to take us both on this surreal outing.

When we arrived at the funeral home, my hands were shaking so hard it was a challenge to turn the car off. I lovingly gazed at Alysia in her little car seat. She was sucking her favorite two fingers and clutching her beloved, yellow blanket. She put her little arms out, and I scooped her up. In we went. I remember vividly every detail of that day.

Why do so many funeral homes need to be redecorated? I find them dark, always cold, and depressing. This one was no exception. Perhaps it is partly because the energy of sorrow is hovering in the corners. We cautiously went into the viewing room. We were frozen in place as we stared at his body. It was dressed in the clothes I had brought the previous day. The flannel sport coat that he loved, and the pale, yellow shirt adorned his body. I immediately noticed, to my horror, that embalming fluid was running down the side of his mouth and onto his shirt! I quickly reached down and wiped it away before Alysia had time to spot it. I was furious that the attention to detail was so lacking. Yuck. This "dead body thing" is just so weird when you actually think about it. We are preserving a body … for what? I decided to hold the thought to ponder later.

I held her in my arms as we stood by the beautiful oak casket. I began telling her again, "Daddy is not sleeping." I touched his chest and told her the story of his heart attack, how it had stopped beating, and the doctors couldn't get it to work again.

She looked at his body and then spent a lot of time looking around the room. After a few moments, she said, "Mommy could we go now?" And that was all there was to that.

She never again asked if he was coming home or where he was. She seemed to accept it and began to move on. Certainly, there were tears at times, and she was a sad little girl for months. For the most part, she moved on in the beautiful way that children do, embracing life in the present moment. It was true … if I were okay then she was okay. In my heart, I knew that one day Alysia would need to retrieve the pieces of her lost childhood and revisit any unexpressed grief.

I was powerless over the increased separation anxiety she would exhibit. I considered this a normal reaction to the loss of a parent. I gave quite an acting performance for my little girl. I was determined to heal for her. I somehow found the stamina to keep putting one foot in front of the other. We were two brave females staring death in the face. Honestly, it would be years before I would feel as if I were a semblance of "put back together."

When we returned home, I phoned the funeral home. I told them the story of bringing my little girl to their establishment and about the fluid dripping out of his mouth. I was frustrated, and I said, "He looks (I searched for the words), he looks so *dead*." I held back the sobs. It sounded so silly. They assured me that they would purchase a new shirt and take care of the problem.

I returned one final time on day three. Roses were the flower that James always bought me, specifically red roses. I went to a florist and bought a single red rose. I had gathered all the cards his children had given him. I also wrote a good-bye letter to him. I tucked these things into his casket. This was my symbolic way of making one last loving gesture. When I left, I felt closure about the physical part of our life. I fully realized there never could be a time when I would be *ready* to let go, no matter the number of years we shared.

As my mind cleared a bit, I began to be acutely aware of the meaningful events surrounding his death. Along with the premonitions he must have been having, there was abundant love and support caressing him. I assume this provided a powerful energy vortex from which he could cross to the next life.

CHAPTER 9

Messages from Beyond

Communication does not stop at the doorway of death. The wall between physical reality and spirit is very thin.

~Emmanuel's Book

The day after his death, I looked in his wallet. As I mindlessly thumbed through the contents, I found the Indian poem about death that we had discussed. I couldn't believe he was actually carrying it around with him. It occurred to me that at some level he was preparing for his own death. He had also been having nightmares that year. James would wake up screaming, "*No!*" He couldn't recall the dreams, but he was certainly resisting something he feared.

A hospice nurse once told me, "You don't live in this body for a lifetime and not know when the end is coming."

The events that followed, I can only assure you are true. If they hadn't happened to me, I would be skeptical myself. I will admit, I have had a fascination with the metaphysical for many years. This has left me with an open mind and a desire to watch and listen for unusual occurrences. I had read books on the subject of life after death and near-death experiences. I interviewed many of my patients regarding their own experiences with loved ones who had crossed over. I heard amazing metaphysical stories which many patients had been reluctant to share with anyone else.

The second night after James' death, my mother arrived from California. Up to this time, my mom was the most psychic member of our family. She often had premonitions and prophetic dreams. Mom was exhausted from the emotional trauma and the trip. She excused herself to retire early. When she hugged me goodnight, I said to her, "I wonder if I'll get a sign."

"I hope so Honey. Goodnight." She seemed to have no idea what I was referring to.

The next morning, I awoke at six and found my mother sitting in the living room. She looked quite pale and upset. "What's wrong Mom?"

"Sherry, I have had an experience unlike any I have ever encountered. I can only imagine that it will make sense to you because I don't understand it at all." I began having rushes up and down my spine. I mean spine tingling, hair raising, physical responses to what she was about to tell me. With wonderment in her voice, she related her experience:

"I was suddenly awakened in the night and I sat upright in bed. I could see in front of me four distinct boxes resembling a hologram. I heard Jim's voice in my mind."

He said, "***Janet, don't be afraid. It's James. She had to have a sign. I don't know why she had to have a sign, but she had to have a sign. Tell her that the sign is green. Janet, I am out here on the court. (We had a sport court.) Really, I am everywhere! I am even in the wind.*** (He was referring to the line in the poem about being in the wind.) ***Don't worry about Sherry, I will stay with her as long as she needs me.***"

My mother said she then heard a sound of wind that was so loud it was as if the roof would blow off! The experience was over as abruptly as it had begun. She stayed up the rest of the night waiting for me to awaken. She was anxious to share the encounter with me. I was *ecstatic*! My love is fine. There *is* life after death. My mom is a very reliable source. I never doubted for a moment the legitimacy of her experience. The one thing that did not make sense to me were the four boxes she saw.

When he said, "The sign is green." This made all the sense in the world. We talked often about the significance of green in our life. His favorite novel was *Green Mansions* by W.H. Hudson. Our house was green as well as the beautiful northwest which we loved. Green is the color of rebirth. The heart chakra is green. We had just put emerald green carpet in our house. I always told him how sexy he looked in his green surgery scrubs. The list went on and on. It seemed he was in a sea of green on the other side. I began to get a sense of a deep inner voice urging me to pay very close attention to everything going on both in me and around me.

The next day, which was day three after his death, I was sitting with my mom at our kitchen table. We were looking out at the back yard. It was the only time Mom and I were alone all week. I had four beautiful flower boxes hanging from the eves along our two large picture windows. I had a local nursery plant flower boxes for us every summer. Suddenly, one of the boxes fell to the ground. I immediately thought, "That's my sign." At once, my logic took over and I assumed the basket had gotten too heavy for the hook. The next day, I went out to pick up the flower box and sort out the debris. I immediately realized that the hook and the eye bolt it was hanging on were perfectly intact. The basket had been lifted off! Once again, I experienced those spine-tingling sensations. I then knew that the four boxes in my mom's vision were the flower baskets hanging on our eves. The event involved flowers much like the story I had told him. Most importantly, it *was* obvious!

Every morning the first week, I would wake up at six with some sort of unusual thoughts or a word in my mind. They did not feel like they were coming from me. It was as if someone just said something in my ear. This was James normal waking hour but not mine. I began to see a pattern emerging.

One morning, the message was "***No organ music! Call Randy***." The only Randy I knew was an oncologist at our clinic. I phoned him and asked if he had anything to do with music. He told me he was a guitarist and had a friend in Seattle who was a professional, classical guitarist. He agreed to enlist him to play for the memorial service. James certainly was adamant about organ music not being played! Eric played beautifully for the service. I was tremendously grateful for each person's contribution to making it so personal. I continue to be amazed at the giving nature of our loving community to reach out in so many thoughtful ways.

Tuesday night, I went to bed and said, "James, if you want me to apply for your veteran's benefit I will need your discharge papers from the Air Force." I had no idea where they would be. I didn't know him then nor if they still existed. I woke up the next morning with the word *"x-rays"* in my mind. I was at a loss to understand what this meant, but I pondered it all day. At some point in the past, I remembered seeing an x-ray folder stuffed in the back of a closet in our guest room. I took it down and looked inside. Along with x-rays from a broken ankle sustained in the military, his *discharge papers* were tucked at the bottom! More chills consumed me.

One of these early summer mornings, Alysia came running into my bedroom. She excitedly said, "Mommy, Mommy, guess what? I just had the most amazing dream! *I saw a beautiful rainbow*." She went on to describe all the colors and how it made her feel special and loved. Our two-year old had never told me about a dream before. Rainbows would become a powerful symbol for both of us. We often played *The Rainbow Song* performed by Kermit the frog on *Sesame Street*.

Another morning message was "**Read The Prophet**." He had given me this book by Kahlil Gibran early in our relationship. He truly loved it. James was quite fond of the writings on love and children. I used a passage from this book for his Memorial Service. It was as if he directed the planning of his final farewell.

We did not belong to a specific church community, yet a friend volunteered to ask her minister to host the service. He graciously agreed. The minister came to see me during this first week. The encounter was tremendously warm and wonderful. He had pounded the pavement talking with people who knew James. He said he wanted to personally get to know him in this way before speaking about him. Toward the end of our visit, the minister asked me what my favorite *Bible* verse was. Immediately it came to me, "*God is love.*" 1John 4:8. He said the verse would be the theme of his Memorial Service. I had written a personal eulogy about James, and he agreed to read it. I felt like the service was everything James wanted.

The other recurrent phenomena manifested as a sound of *rustling*. I can only compare it to the sound of static electricity coupled with a feeling of a spirit's presence in the room. This happened a handful of times. It was usually following or during a social gathering of friends when he was being remembered fondly. At one such dinner party, which included a group of fellow surgeons, I was telling them of this sound. As soon as the story was over, the electrical sound came loudly from the kitchen. The group of doctors described having the hair stand up on their arms in that moment!

My dad came to stay with me, and he had his own unnerving experience. He was awakened in the night as if his big toe were being pulled. It happened repeatedly, and each time he went back to sleep. Finally, he decided to get up. When he went into the dining room, the glasses on the wine rack were clanking against each other. He could feel James' presence in the room. He was certain James was playing a joke on him. It rattled him so badly he wouldn't stay in the house.

Most of the people in our life had some sort of mystical experience that they believed were messages from James. Our baby sitter told me she was awakened during the night by her phone ringing. She answered it and heard James' voice on the other end. He said, "Sharon, thank you for taking such good care of our little girl." Catrina said she could hear a heartbeat while she was talking on the phone to me.

Many of his fellow physicians told me that he came to them in their dreams. Several of them felt he was letting them know he was close. Linda, our medical assistant, came to stay at our home. She reported seeing an apparition of James standing in an upstairs window. Our community was profoundly affected by his sudden death. These encounters served to help us process our relationships with him. I believe, more importantly, they were his way of finishing his earth life. He seemed to be reassuring all of us that he had survived his transition.

On day seven, we had a Memorial Service and a party at our home for all of our good friends and family. We had his favorite food and drink and toasted his winning and loving personality. During the service, the minister made a statement I have never forgotten. He said, "Those of you who do not believe in life after death have reason to grieve." I got psychic rushes realizing I had been given the gift of *knowing* there was more. I stood at the exit door and thanked each person in attendance. I was deeply moved by the love and sorrow shining in their eyes. My life felt empty of his physical presence yet full of the legacy of love in our lives.

He often said, "Alysia has a survivor's will." He sincerely wanted me to have this little girl. He left his love for me streaming through her.

Three weeks after his death, I went with Dick and Lynn to our river property. I knew it was time to face what had transpired the day of his death. Upon our arrival, it became quite clear his energy was present. We talked about him and told stories. We could hear footsteps on the deck all around us. His presence was palpable.

When I went to bed that night, my room was filled with his energy. I quietly lay there thinking about him. I was acutely aware of his closeness. I started to feel a sensation of warmth and love infuse my body. I realized it was the energy of lovemaking. He made love to me ... one last time ... spirit to flesh. I allowed it to consume me as our energies melded. I knew it would only happen once, and I didn't miss a moment of the transpersonal experience. I mused that if I had a sudden death and had the ability to communicate, I would want my loved ones to be listening!

Six weeks later, when the most intense emotional pain was beginning to subside, I had my first face on dream encounter with James. He came to me as I was in an aware and conscious state:

He looked younger (about thirty) and androgynous. At first, I wondered if he were gay? I was confused, and then I realized that there is no sexual identity on the other side. He was definitely male in appearance. He had on a white shirt and he glowed, white light emanating around and through him. We immediately embraced. It felt like a long-awaited uniting of our love. After this special embrace, he was excited to tell me, "Sherry, there is God and God is love! You will love again." I said, "What about

Alysia?" He seemed upset by this question and said he would get back to me on that. I could see he was upset at leaving her. He told me that I was on the right path with my metaphysical studies. Following this encounter, I went up steps to an ancient looking building with pillars. There was a large library book stand with a massive book on it. The book was open, and I looked down and saw two words ... patience and perseverance. There was also another love watching me, a male with distinctive blue eyes.

I was definitely lucid while having the experience. The dream was in technicolor, and I knew it was a visitation from my husband. This man, who was a skeptic regarding life after death or the existence of the *Divine*, was setting the record straight! I was deeply humbled to have received the gift of truth from him. From this encounter forward, my spiritual life was changed. I no longer needed to rely on faith in things unseen. I now knew life was eternal and *God* was at the helm.

There was often a presence in our home. I could tell Alysia was aware of it. Other visitors had experiences. Porch lights would come on and off. Glasses continued to clank together. James had a ritual with Alysia. He loved marches. He would play them and march around the house with her. One evening, I played a record of marches for her. We talked about how much fun it had been for them both. After the music was over, the sound of a trumpet blowing filled the room! She would often take a step back as if she saw or felt something. I was not afraid. I found his presence comforting.

One night, Ann and Linda were visiting. Alysia and I were also in the room. Spontaneously, there appeared in the corner of the room a green orb of light. I laughed knowingly and told them James was visiting.

I felt his presence for about three months. He remained close, and I believe helped me when he could. Over the years, he has come to me on occasion in dreams. Always, it is this loving special friend checking in. It became obvious to me that our love was eternal and did in fact continue to grow and expand. I sorely missed my best friend.

My heart was so open. Sudden death is both cruel and a blessing. I felt cheated out of the opportunity for closure. The shock was mind blowing. I felt dissociated from myself as I went through each day.

I was given a dream: *I was allowed one last day with my love. I had and an opportunity to say good-bye. It was the most painful experience imaginable. I awoke feeling immense gratitude that his leaving was sudden. I knew I was strong and courageous enough to move forward without a parting scene of painful good-byes.*

I felt united with *God* through my *Higher Self.* It was as if I were lifted and carried through the entire experience. What I believed was my entire life turned out to be a ten- year chapter. I took solace in the fact that I gave all to love. I know our love is deep and forever.

James fulfilled his promise to let me know if there was life after death. Once I allowed myself to believe that he existed beyond the physical, I could feel intimately connected to him. I was quite aware of a lifting of grief as I became more intrigued by the fact that I now knew there was so much more beyond this life. I had stepped firmly onto my spiritual path.

CHAPTER 10

Life is Calling

Allow yourselves to renew your commitment to your lives and to yourselves many times a day.

~Emmanuel's Book

I felt like I was living in a cocoon of *Divine* protection. I was in front of our home watering the garden. It was one of those special summer mornings. It had been two weeks since her Daddy died. Alysia was with me, and she wanted to go get a toy in the house. Rarely letting her out of my sight, I said, "Hurry back." Soon I began to have a feeling of dread.

About that time, she came running out of the house soaking wet. She was sobbing. She cried, "I fell in the swimming pool and I went to the bottom. I saw the stairs, but I don't know how I got out." I was in shock. She did not know how to swim and furthermore, how did she get into the swimming pool so fast? I believed it was fenced off, yet she somehow squeezed through the gate, probably retrieving a toy. I assumed her guardian angel had reached down to save her. Perhaps *God* in his/her infinite wisdom knew I couldn't deal with another traumatic loss so soon. At any rate, it felt like *Divine* intervention. The event jolted me into being more present. I began taking extra precautions where

74

our safety was concerned. Deep gratitude doesn't even begin to express how I felt. The next day, I had a new pool cover installed, completely sealing it up.

I remember the first time I was introduced as a *widow*. I deplored my new title. Grief left me feeling much older than my thirty years. I desperately wanted to feel vibrant again. It was a dilemma. I began to feel like a third wheel with my married friends and quite out of place with my single ones. I could have used a good therapist, at the time, to help me sort through these feelings. I was fiercely independent, and foolishly believed I could manage my affairs on my own. I knew I had to move on with my life. I was acutely aware of the secondary losses associated with losing my mate. Nothing in my life was the same.

Eventually, I started dating. I found the divorced men either immature or angry. There were no internet dating sites at the time. I was dependent on friends to send eligible men my way. This was merely a distraction from my grief.

My roommate from nursing school, Toni, came to visit me. We were very close. She was a surgical nurse and had worked with James. She was anxious to share an experience. Toni said she had been concerned because I did not belong to a church community of any kind. She had been in a prayer circle that met weekly. While in prayer and meditation, she received a vision: Toni saw cupped hands come before her and a voice said quite clearly, "***The widow is in my hands. She will***

walk the streets of gold with you." Toni told me she would stop worrying!

Quite frankly, I was afraid to let myself go to the depths of the pain. I continued to put on a brave act for Alysia. After about four months, I was scheduled for a hysterectomy. Without the responsibility of parenting and a household to take care of, I let down emotionally. My surgeon told the nurses to keep visitors out and allow me to grieve. I cried for twenty-four hours straight. The experience was transformative and cathartic. It really helped to rebalance my emotions. During the night, as I was suffering physically and emotionally, I could feel James in the room. I heard the characteristic *rustling* sound. His energy seemed unsettled.

The next day, Ann came in to tell me of an experience. *During the night, she had a lucid dream. Her Dr. Scott came to her and he was upset and conveyed that he wanted to be with me. She said, "No! Alysia needs her mother. Go away."* He definitely made his presence known to many who were open channels.

One of my friends commented that I would be a hard act to follow. She said I had been so courageous. Yes, indeed I projected strength, yet on the inside I was devastated and unsure of myself. I returned to my position as a nurse practitioner. I was suffering from severe post-traumatic stress. Words would swim on the page as I attempted to do the simplest of tasks. My brain was in a major fog. I decided I needed more time.

My independence cost me financially. I had a couple of experiences when criminals set out to take advantage of my vulnerability. One firm actually read the obituaries and scammed me by telling me my husband had asked them for a bid to replace our roof. James and I had previously discussed replacing the roof. This made the entire experience believable at first. I gave them the job and a large sum of money, only to lose it in the end. Looking back, I would have done well to enlist the guidance of trusted friends when making large decisions. I was driven by my compulsion to complete James' unfinished business.

I was graced with a great attorney referral. He saw to it that my legal rights and affairs were in order. This can be a very real and stressful part of moving on. Blended families have special issues to deal with when dividing an estate. My husband thought his affairs were in order, but they were not. This was added stress none of us needed. Thankfully, we sorted it all out in the end.

I found it extremely difficult to get through my long days without a crutch. My emotions would surface around four every day. I turned to my seductive bottle of wine. As families settled in for dinner, I was just beginning each long and lonely night. Alysia was my salvation. While almost everything in my life had changed, she was the one constant. She still needed consistent love and attention. This gave my life structure, meaning, and purpose. One night a clear voice in my mind said, "***Continue the drinking and*** *you will soon become addicted*." I knew it was true. I did not want to put Alysia through any more trauma. I began to curtail the self-medicating use of alcohol. I journaled daily, and I read every book I could find on grief and moving on. A cardinal rule was to feel your feelings, avoid alcohol and other mood-altering substances because use of them only slows down the process of grief.

I simply faked it until I actually did feel better. I focused on all the blessings in my life. I empathized with survivors who had so little at a time like this. I saw my plight as an opportunity for growth at many levels. I felt a powerful rebirthing time coming upon me. I reconnected with my past and made amends wherever needed.

It was years before Alysia slept through the night. She needed reassurance that I was alive and well. One night, I asked her what was waking her up. She said, "Mommy, I'm afraid you will die like Daddy did." If you want to know the truth of a situation, just ask a two-year old. I reassured her that even though I could not promise, I planned on living for a long time.

I am eternally grateful for the multitude of good friends who took time out of their own lives to bolster me. I felt very loved. This started me on my healing journey. Chris brought books on children and grief. Catrina signed me up for her soccer league. Teresa occupied me with long daily walks and talks.

Toni accompanied me on a ski bus weekly that first winter. Dick and Lynn took me to the ocean and on many outings. My close friends provided much needed distractions and healing experiences outdoors. They invited me to social gatherings and play dates for the kids. Through their generosity and compassion, they helped me remember that I had intrinsic value without being a wife, a nurse, or a mother. These special earth angels were love in action.

Gratitude became the most powerful tool in my life skills toolbox. Counting my blessings; past, present, small and large, kept me afloat. I realized that what I focused on would grow. Surges of feeling thankful helped me be optimistic, gain my footing, and eased my suffering during this transition time.

On James first birthday following his death, I was having a very emotional day. I apologized to Alysia and told her I was sad because I missed Daddy, and it was his birthday. This wise little three-year-old said, "But Mommy, it's 1982 and Daddy doesn't need any more birthdays." This was the exact perspective I needed.

Emotional support was showered upon me. I asked *God* to guide me, protect me, and light my path. I desperately wanted someone to love and to have a family again. I was still youthful and believed I was ready to begin a new chapter.

I knew that because of this life experience, I would be able to help others someday. I was acutely aware of the continuum of love in my life and the many forms it was taking. In its simplest equation, death has only one thing to impart ... *Love is always the lesson.*

After the recommended year mark, I chose to sell our home. Alysia and I moved back to my hometown in California where my family of origin was residing. I assumed the family connections would be good for both of us. I surrendered my life to *God* and took the next indicated step.

PART TWO

CHAPTER 11

Out of the Frying Pan

We must be willing to let go of the life we planned as to have the life that is waiting for us.

~Joseph Campbell

Have you ever tried to be in a relationship with a porcupine? It's tricky to say the least. The best word to describe both the man and the life we shared … *complicated.* Soon I would embark on a compelling karmic relationship. I was attracted to a man who had a complex personality disorder. This no doubt resulted from genetics plus the extreme conditions of his childhood. The entire situation was a conundrum. Providence brought us together. I was admittedly lonely and eager for adult companionship. I am definitely a relationship person. It's where my spiritual growth happens.

My Washington life was behind me. The excitement of the return to my home town was waning. I wanted a new beginning and most of all, yearned for family life. I prayed for guidance daily. I consciously surrendered my life to *God's* plan. I made a pact with my *Divine Source*. "Please give me someone to love. I will allow you to lead the way." Once again, I created my own reality.

I had a bad tire on my car. I made several calls from the *Yellow Pages* to have it taken care of. I'm not certain why I made a third inquiry but when Bobby's voice came on the line, I felt the familiar psychic rush. This lead me to be very curious about the man on the other end. He brusquely told me if I had ten minutes, he could take care of the problem. Well I did have ten minutes. (As it came to pass, I had the rest of my life to spend with this man.) I strapped Alysia in her car seat, and to the tire shop we went. Years later, he would admit he made more money on that used tire than he would have on a new Michelin! The man, I thought at the time was so honest, was in reality a master manipulator.

I remember how hot the day was. Summer was drawing to a close. Fall, my favorite season, was in the air. I was weary from my year as a widow. The daily duties of parenting my busy, intelligent little girl gave me purpose. Even though I had tried dating, I had not included her in the experience. I intended to keep that part of my life private until a serious suitor came along. Every day, she begged and pleaded for a daddy. I would chuckle and say, "I can't just go get one at the Blue Light Special at K-mart." I grieved for my life in Washington, although in my home-town I did feel safe and nurtured by my family. This was where I belonged for now. I knew the universe was working out all the other details.

As I waited for my tire change, I watched this interesting man work his magic on his customers. I detected an east coast accent. Even though he was very busy, he connected with me right away. This guy was quite an entertaining character. Bobby had a joke for each person and enough energy for three men. He was hyperactive to be sure! He was directing his employees, ringing up customers, and answering three lines on the phone: all at the same time. The laziness of grief had consumed me. His energy was a sharp contrast to my mental state. I was mostly taken by his sense of humor. This was incredibly refreshing compared to my year of heaviness.

His sense of humor would be the saving grace of our entire life together. During the best and the worst of times, there was always a place for comedic relief. I immediately loved his passionate spirit. He was a New Yorker through and through. Growing up in an Italian neighborhood in Queens, we could not have been more opposite. I'm a California Valley girl raised on a ranch and in small towns. We called ourselves *country mouse* and *city mouse*. This often created totally different perceptions of life.

I went to the counter to pay my bill not thinking he had even noticed me. I would eventually discover that this guy never missed a detail in life. His ability to hyper-focus was survival for him. He queried, "I see you have Washington plates on your car. Did your husband get transferred here?" I responded with a matter of fact tone, "No he's *dead*." He said, "I am going through a divorce. I think that's worse." I laughed, wondering how he could possibly know which loss was greater. My bluntness didn't faze him, and his audacity failed to affect me.

He followed me out to my car, and suddenly he seemed very boyish and unsure of himself. These were his exact words to me: "I have never asked out a customer, but would you like to have dinner some night?" I told him dinner sounded nice, and he promised to phone. That brief glimpse of shyness was the only time in my eighteen years with him that I saw such a quality.

He rang me up that very night. We talked non-stop for two hours. I needed to get Alysia to bed but, I was intrigued by the direction our visit was going. I invited him over to finish the conversation. I was anxious to have the male companionship, and admittedly I was hungry for the attention. We covered an immense amount of material that night, each of us willing to bare our souls. In the beginning, our ego boundaries were down. We gazed directly into each other's souls. It was incredible. I would spend years trying to find my way back to that place.

Alysia was also quite taken with the tall dark Italian. He showered both of us with thoughtful gifts. His arrival after work was always an adventure. He kept me in fresh flowers and poetry. We went out to dinner the next night and every night after that. It was a special time for sharing our hopes and dreams. We were very different, yet we had a mutual vision for our future. *Family first* was our motto. His passion for life, his wit, and emotional depth were so attractive to me. His New York background and strong Italian identity piqued my curiosity. He was fun, and we had enormous good times together. I knew right away that I was the pot of gold at the end of his rainbow. It felt wonderful to be embraced and appreciated so enthusiastically.

At the time, I believed this man was the answer to my prayers. He wanted a family to love and nurture as much as I did. The third night after our meeting, he had a dream. He called me to share. He said he was walking through a sea of *green*, totally immersed in the color. I had not told him the significance of green to me. I really believed this was a signpost meant to reassure me I was on the right path. He had a copy of *Green Mansions* and also *The Prophet* on his bookshelf. (The books James gave to me.) The early period in our relationship was rich with meaningful content. He filled our life with rainbows and gave a fatherless little girl a daddy to love. This man had a magnificent and powerful spirit.

He would be inspired to scribe poetry quite spontaneously. I had many chills when I read this first poem he composed for me:

We have evolved from another life
To meet this moment
In this life and time
A life and time where love
"Lasting love"
Goes against the grain.
We ... by Divine appointment have
Once again been placed on earth
To (by example) save a world where
Love is becoming but a vague image
Of what we left before.
So once again we meet
And hand in hand
We'll begin our journey.
You're more beautiful than I remember.
I've missed you!

He took me to New York to show me where he grew up. We rode the subway out to Queens. It was an unfamiliar environment to me. The trip triggered many memories for him. I began to get a very clear picture of just how deep his shadow world was. I felt empathy for him. What would have been a red flag for most, only drew me in deeper.

I experienced a true metaphysical connection with Bobby even though his ways were quite foreign to me. I saw telltale signs of the dark side of his passion. It was clear that he needed to be in control of his life. He was easily frustrated when things did not turn out the way he expected, and he was quite thin-skinned.

Bobby shared with me that he had been seeing a therapist. He wanted me to meet him. I respected the fact that he cared enough about his life to seek professional guidance. I eagerly accompanied him on his next visit. The therapist turned out to be a very wise and loving soul. He was well trained in family counseling and quite intuitive as well. The doctor encouraged us regarding the future of our relationship. I totally trusted him. I might have been better off to trust my own instincts more.

Bobby believed he had finally arrived in the right life. He stopped going for those very important weekly sessions. This should have been another serious warning sign. I was enjoying my day to day life with him. I wasn't willing to look deeper for potential problems. Making a *decision* to love was much different than my experience with James. I had my little family, and I was determined to do my part in making it a loving, lasting one.

Bobby had remained friends with his first wife of many years. She was the reason he had originally moved to California. He insisted we meet. She seemed a lovely woman and very mild mannered. They were married in their teens and had an amicable divorce. It was apparent to me that they still loved each other in a familial way. She was a Madonna figure for him. When he was frustrated with me, he would tell me I should be more like her. She played the unconditional loving parent role for him. He might as well have asked, "Will you love me and be my mother?" Many psychology books later … I figured this out.

We both had baggage, and we were extremely honest about our families, past lives, and marriages. It was time for a fresh start. I told him of my love for James. The true joy in his life was his seven-month old son. It was unusual to meet a man with a baby. I will never forget the day he brought baby Sam to meet us. I fell in love with this blue-eyed baby boy long before I fell in love with his daddy. Alysia was thrilled to have a baby to love. It was what we both needed at the time. I treasured my time with the kids. Mothering is what made me whole. Sam was the greatest, unexpected gift life has ever given me.

I fostered a relationship with Sam's mom, Bobby's second wife. This wasn't easy with a baby. I promised I would take good care of him during our shared time. I further assured her, "I will never try to take your place." We regularly found ourselves navigating the turbulent waters of divorce and joint custody. This became the central theme in our lives. Eventually, Lynn and I became friends. We both realized that life with Bobby could be like walking through a minefield. He did his best to respect her as Sam's mom. Effective communication was often a struggle for them both.

I was committed to always consider and represent, what I believed, were the best interests of this child. Little Sam and I bonded quickly. My love for him surprised me. He is a sweet, imaginative, and loving spirit. I could not have felt more connected if he had come through my body. I was honored to help raise him and be his *Mama Sherry*.

Bobby was a very emotional man. His life was full of extreme highs and lows. He was able to use the skills learned in counseling to grow through each crisis he faced. In the beginning, this was impressive. He had an uncanny ability to read people. Life in the ghetto had required unique survival skills. I was not accustomed to a relationship so full of extremes. I admit, it made me uncomfortable, yet I told myself this is what life with a passionate man looks like.

I knew of his childhood wounds. Along with having very dysfunctional parents, at the age of four he spent a year in the hospital recovering from rheumatic fever. This prolonged institutional experience was devastating. He could remember children dying and how he was abandoned for long periods of time. I would soon discover, this left him with phobias and numerous dysfunctional habits. He told stories of mobsters and what life on the streets had been like.

Bobby wore his wounds on his sleeve. In the beginning, he seemed able to bask in the glow of the children's unconditional love. This was salve to his wounds and an answer to his prayers. I reflected on my own dysfunctional family history, and it seemed quite tame by comparison.

As for me, I was the perfect caretaking, co-dependent lover. I convinced myself that unconditional love would heal his wounds. I chose to believe we would live happily-ever-after. This is what we both desperately wanted. As it turned out, I had a serious case of the Helper's Disease and naivety beyond belief. I was in way over my head. We were mutually willing to take risks. As a result, we had daily opportunities to learn. He was a tremendous teacher in so many ways.

Bobby was also quite the talker. Our conversations were both stimulating and profound. He used to say, "When we take a car trip, we have to drive around the hotel twice, when we arrive, just to finish the conversation."

I once attended a class where we meditated on what fairy tale character we identified with. My subconscious quickly spit out *Fairy Godmother*. I *really* believed I could wave my magic wand and make his dreams come true.

It took some time for me to fall in love with Bobby. I came home the second week of dating him to find a mountain of his clothes thrown on the floor of my entry hall. I knew he was testing me. He doubted I would actually accept him into my life. There wasn't a day that he didn't test my love. The die was cast. Against my better judgement, I hung them up in the closet. He called to see what I had done with his clothes, and I told him where they were. He simply said, "I wanted to see what you would do." We never discussed his bold act again.

From that day forward, we were a couple. Our lives quickly became enmeshed. Eight months later, we went to Scotland and were married at *Gretna Green*. It was all very romantic and a fun adventure. On our wedding trip, I realized he had debilitating panic attacks. He called them his monsters controlling him with fear, anger, and guilt from his past.

One morning, after we returned from Scotland, I sat sipping tea on the patio. As I basked in the warmth of the early summer sun, I closed my eyes to meditate. Immediately, my consciousness was in an expanded state of awareness. I was no longer confined to my physical body. The experience of atonement was remarkable. I was able to rest in this altered state for several minutes. This realization was followed by a clear voice speaking in my mind, ***"This is the peace that passes all understanding."*** *(*From Philippians 4:7) I had prayed for peace and understanding when James died. I now knew in my soul that I was in the life predestined for me. I felt safe in the knowledge that *God* would protect my heart.

In spite of my spiritual understanding, my instincts were telling me this was not going to be an easy life. By the time we married, the honeymoon phase was already wearing off. We were now dealing with real life issues.

My parents were not convinced we were a good match. Their concern and unease helped to create a continual crisis in the family. Bobby couldn't handle rejection. My Mom and Dad couldn't deal with his emotional approach to life. I was constantly in the middle. Looking back, I believe I was still numb from the loss of James. Being with Bobby made me feel alive again.

We met with my estate attorney to have a living trust agreement drawn up. My attorney strongly recommended we draw up a pre-nuptial agreement as well. Bobby was quite willing and mature about the advice. For years after, he berated me for signing it. Without my knowledge, it had hurt him greatly. For me, it was purely an academic exercise because I am not a quitter, and I never wanted to go through a divorce.

Bobby desperately wanted to adopt Alysia. A one year waiting period was required for a step-parent adoption. We went to see our family therapist and took Alysia with us. She chose to sit on his lap during the session. The doctor observed, "You can't fool children, and this little girl wants Bobby to be her daddy." I put all my money on one hand, realizing it was a gamble. I made the decision to fully commit to our newly formed family and to the man I believed loved me with all his heart. Truthfully, he wanted to love with all his heart. Unfortunately, his heart was deeply wounded. I would love him without measure, choosing to believe that this was my destiny.

CHAPTER 12

Relationship Angst

The family is a hothouse for spiritual growth.

~Emmanuel's Book

Moving forward, we spent most of our time with our children and their various activities. We both loved parenting. We lived in a bubble of affection and love for our new family. For the first several years, life was reasonably manageable, joyful, and happy.

It didn't take long before I began to notice a pattern. Bobby would create crises over the smallest of incidents. It became evident that he was quite comfortable with chaos. In fact, he thrived on it. I was the opposite. *Peace at any price* was my thing. His need to control everyone and everything in his life was near addiction. He had other compulsive, self-destructive habits, including bulimia and smoking. Bobby had very high expectations for himself and all those around him.

As the years unfolded, I realized how unforgiving a person he was. He was somewhat paranoid as well. With few exceptions, holding on to friendships was impossible. The people in our life came and went through his revolving door. He was fond of saying that I had to take him everywhere twice, the second time to apologize. I can tell you that in eighteen years I rarely had any peace, always waiting for the other shoe to drop. I loved our family in spite of my misgivings about our future. I refused to be intimidated by his shadow traits. When triggered, he was coercive and combative.

I began to feel like I was treading water. I would be pulled under without warning. I always fought my way to the surface. Every day started the same. We consistently enjoyed happy and loving mornings which brought hopefulness to the day. By afternoon, his emotional body would take control, and life became very unpredictable. In the early years, the conflicts were usually about outsiders. This would eventually change. As his love for his family grew, so did his fear of losing us.

Due to his symptomatology, I became suspicious of a personality disorder. I was constantly explaining his irrational behavior to the kids. I would try to help them understand when he was being reasonable versus unrealistic in his expectations of them. He over-parented and micromanaged every aspect of our lives. To him, this was what a loving responsible parent was required to do. He was dedicated beyond belief. I have no doubt he was giving them the childhood he never had.

Truth be told, I had a tiger by the tail! I had grown to deeply love my tiger in spite of his emotional make-up. Understanding him did help. He was extremely intelligent but not formally educated. He wanted this life we were creating yet had such deep emotional scars. He would spend a lifetime trying to figure out how to get love that was inside of him all the time. Bobby needed constant reassurance of our love. My saving grace was my professional background, my love for myself, and my ability to recognize the insanity when it surfaced. I am a very forgiving person. This ability was put to the test most days. After a time, I learned not to judge him and then forgiveness wasn't necessary. An abundance of *patience* and *perseverance* was mandatory for the survival of our family. I feared it would be very damaging for the kids if they had to deal with him alone. Many days, I felt like I was living with three children. Our ideas of what was acceptable, conventional behavior were quite different. The light at the end of my tunnel was an oncoming train!

We ended each day of our eighteen years together with, "Thank you *God.*" We took time to reflect on all that was good in our day and our life. Some days it was hard to feel sincere, but I daily saw the evidence that our relationship was founded on the spiritual principal of gratitude. This saved us during some very rough storms. I searched for the good in every day. Continually, we found things to love about each other.

My logic questioned my decision to be with him, yet my heart urged me on. In the face of frequent adversity, I became stronger and more resilient. I continued to believe in the power of love and commitment. I would dig in my heels and be loving each time the testing and intimidation would ensue. There was genuine laughter and affection at some point in each and every day. I attributed this to our ability to step outside of our ego dramas and gain perspective. This offered a brief respite from the emotional storms passing through.

He depended on me for everything emotional in his life. Bobby told me he thought I was so stable and loving that we could overcome any rough spots in the road. He would do anything to protect his family. Over the years, his endless need for attention became exhausting. He told me he couldn't handle the toilet paper roll going the wrong way, but he could deal with big traumas. The emotional climate in our home could change from hour to hour.

The qualities he loved in me when we were first together, became the qualities he grew to resent. He became intimidated by my education. I would feel uncomfortable and know that a situation was toxic. He would try and convince me it didn't happen that way. He would embellish and fabricate stories to affect an outcome. This often left me feeling confused. At times, I doubted my own sanity. For a time, my self-confidence suffered a noticeable setback.

For years, there was a common denominator involved in his worst outbursts. This was alcohol. The more he drank, the more irrational he became. He was downright nasty when he had more than a drink in him. Bobby would exhibit a different, more desperate personality. He became thoughtless, insensitive, and sometimes mean-spirited. The following day, he had no memory of these outbursts. I would eventually realize, he was dissociating when he drank. It was impossible to hold him accountable when he had zero recollection of his behavior. The following day, we would be back to our loving, fun, and adventurous life.

Early in our relationship, I saw a flash of anger directed at me. I had the thought, "This man could be abusive." I had never intimately known an aggressive man, so a degree of denial and self-deception was natural. I woke up the next morning, and I could barely walk to the bathroom. I was in excruciating pain. I dropped my gown and was horrified at what I saw. My back was deeply bruised as if I had been beaten with a board. At once, I knew my body had stored a painful memory from a past life with him. It had surfaced when I realized his potential for abuse. I vowed never to provoke him. My inner guidance encouraged me to love myself and my family. I continued on the relationship path I had chosen, inwardly questioning my decision. Strange as it may sound, I knew in my heart that a karmic debt was being repaid here.

My understanding of the complexities of dysfunctional relationships grew. I began to read every psychology book I could get my hands on. He lived on every page. It took many years for me to understand he had borderline personality disorder. More and more, I was walking on eggshells. He was high functioning yet a classic borderline. I remained idealistic in my thinking. Had I known the challenges commitment would bring, I doubt I would have had the courage. I was acutely aware of the fact that this man was not his wounds. Lack of loving role models had certainly left its path of destruction. He guessed at what normal was and clearly didn't have a clue much of the time.

As the relationship unfolded, I became more co-dependent. This is likely the reason I made an excellent nurse. Inventory taking was my special skill. A complex script of manipulation evolved between us. I treasured the times when we could relax and be authentic and loving.

In meditation, I asked my Higher Self to show me a significant past life with Bobby: *I was immediately on a carpet ride! I looked down off the carpet into a courtyard. There was a mosque and I am aware it is somewhere in the Middle East. Suddenly, I am standing in the courtyard and holding the tether of a camel. I can even smell the camel. I know I am waiting for my husband. Out walks Bobby. I am certain it is him. He is dressed in black leather and is carrying a whip. He is quite an imposing figure, large and cruel. I have a veil across my face. I know that I am part of his harem and that he abuses me. My guidance told me that my mother in this past life is my mother now. She was sorely afraid for me, praying constantly for my protection. I realize that her distrust of him runs deep, emanating from that time. My soul memory of his power over me began to clarify my awareness of my difficult path.*

Soon after, I had a past life vision of a time when I had abused him. Our past lives were about forgiveness. I pondered this revelation for a long time.

Sam also had a past life memory. *From the time he was about four, he would say that he was my champion and he had fought for me in a different life. He would tell his dad that I belonged to him!* He was quite adamant about it, complete with a colorful description of this time.

I had many dreams working out the complexities of the situation. *The most profound experience in my dream world was a visitation from Jesus. He sat on the edge of my bed, touched my forehead quite gently, and said to me,* **"I am always with you."**

I also dreamed of James often. On my birthday, I walked by a wall clock of his which had not run since his death. It began to chime! I missed him so much. I was aware of the evolution of my love for him and of his presence from time to time. More and more, I looked within for direction and guidance.

CHAPTER 13

Mental Illness

The wound is the place where the light enters you.

~Rumi

Our birth experience and subsequent relationship with our first love, our mother, lays the foundation for trust. From our subconscious mind, our inner child directs our life script. I believe the way a man relates to the women in his life is tied to these early experiences. My compassion and understanding of Bobby was enhanced by meeting and experiencing his mother. Nothing in my background or education would prepare me for dealing with this demented woman.

In New York, Bobby's mother was known as *Queenie*. She ruled her home and all who were unfortunate enough to come into her world with an unkind iron fist. It was widely known that she was totally narcissistic and abusive. This mother and son had a history of spending years estranged. He had no love loss or respect for her. Bobby described a woman who had been controlling, punitive, and distant when he was a child. She also had been in and out of mental institutions for diagnosed schizophrenia.

About five years into our marriage, she called and apologized to him. She wanted to reconnect. She oozed sincerity. He was understandably suspicious yet decided to move forward and give her another chance. He was so proud of our family and of his life. He wanted her approval in the worst way. Magical thinking is easy in these situations. I wanted him to be able to forgive his past. Bobby convinced her to fly out and meet all of us. Bobby had adopted Alysia a year into our marriage. He wanted his mom to meet both of the kids. She said she was afraid to fly and would only come if he escorted her. He reluctantly agreed.

When she arrived, I had our home all warm and cozy. It was during the holidays, and she planned to stay for three months. The timeline was her idea. Bobby introduced her to me and to Alysia who was seven at the time. She was syrupy sweet to us. She sat down at the kitchen table and *ordered* me to sit next to her. She proceeded to bring out a jewelry box and set it on the table. She crooned, "These are my most precious jewels. You are my only living son's wife. I want you to have them."

I started to protest that she should keep them for herself. She seemed agitated, "No! I insist that you have them. I can't wear them in New York. I would most certainly get mugged. They are only sitting in a safety deposit box. You must have them with my blessings. Now put them on." There was a lovely pearl necklace and a diamond ring as well as an onyx ring. They were beautiful pieces. I carefully put them on. I hugged her and thanked her profusely. I told her that

I would treasure her gifts always. I was beginning to have a feeling of foreboding. This encounter was quite unusual.

Bobby excused himself from the room to attend to a phone call. As soon as he was out of ear shot, her demeanor changed dramatically. A hateful look came over her, and she grabbed my arm digging her nails into my skin. She emphatically said, "Listen Dearie, my son likes your daughter well enough, but in my family, we worship our own blood. Don't you ever forget that!" About that time, Bobby came back into the room. She resumed her sweet motherly attitude toward us. I felt totally disoriented. It was that feeling of confusion you get when you are being lied to.

I was in shock. My skin was crawling with this creepy feeling that an evil force had entered our lives. I knew I would have to watch her very carefully. I had experience in a mental institution during my nurse's training. She closely resembled some of the patients I had worked with. I told Bobby about the encounter. He insisted he would set her straight. He said she was not going to come into our home and start disrupting our happy life. I begged him to let it go this time. He decided to hold his tongue, but we were both quite guarded. I did make certain that she had brought her psychiatric medications. She assured us she was taking them.

The first week went pretty smooth. We introduced her to my extended family and showed her around the town. The weather was mild, and she would go out walking during the day. I asked her to tell me about her childhood. I was hoping to get some clues regarding her mental state. She told me of her very large family and a father who came home drunk daily and beat her mother. One day her older brother beat her father. He told him he would kill him if he ever touched their mother again. I began to feel some empathy for her. The story depicts the extreme dysfunction in this family's history. I realized she had very deep psychological wounds. As a result, she had in turn inflicted wounds on her children.

The next morning, we walked into her room and found her bed covered with dollar bills. She asked me to take a picture of her covered in money. "I want to send it to my friends in New York. I will tell them that my Bobby gave me all this money when I arrived." I was beginning to get the picture of her mental state. Next, she wanted us to drive her to a lovely house she had seen on one of her walks and take a picture of her in front of it. She said she wanted to send that picture back to New York. She intended to tell her friends that we lived in this house because it was so much better than the house we did live in! Believe me, our home was beautiful. She asked to be taken to the bank. She wanted to open a savings account for Sam and deposit money in it. Bobby told her he had two children, and she had two grandchildren. She must treat them equally.

She refused, saying she really only had one grandchild because of the blood thing.

Bobby was quite angry. He sat her down and confronted her about her behavior. "You have done this to me my entire life. You have always gone out of your way to try and make me feel unimportant. Why? I will not tolerate this nastiness in my own home." They argued for a time, and then she pulled a copy of her will out of her purse. She told him she was going to write him out of it. He took it out of her hands and tore it up. She demanded the gifted jewelry back. He said, "No way. The jewelry was a gift to my wife. I will not humiliate myself to honor your crazy requests." Yikes! Our time with her was getting more insane by the day. My anxiety level was climbing steadily.

Following this outburst, she locked herself in her bedroom and refused to eat. We could hear her engaging in imaginary conversations. She was obviously having hallucinations. I felt sorry for her. I also respected the power of mental illness. I was actually locking my bedroom door at night. Due to her jealousy of Bobby's love for us, her projected hatred was being directed at me. I could see that she was going through my personal things when we left the house, undoubtedly looking for the jewelry. I wanted to give it back to her, but Bobby refused.

She lost an extreme amount of weight. We finally convinced her to go home and proceeded to change her flight date. The night before she left, she was roaming the house and tripped over the coffee table and fell. I could hear her screaming, "That woman is trying to kill me!" Meaning me, of course. It was such a nightmarish time for all of us. There was no way to turn her around. I was certain she had stopped taking her prescriptions. The best thing we could do was get her home to her familiar world where she had control. She was with us for three long weeks.

All communication had ceased, and she stone-walled us. She continued to refuse food. *Queenie* pranced onto that airplane without a good-bye or a look back. When she arrived home, she went straight to her attorney and had him change her will. She also had him send a letter from his office accusing us of abusing her. She demanded the return of all the jewelry and money she had given Sam. Bobby was furious and humiliated. He called the attorney and told him the truth of what had really transpired. He was adamant about the fact that we would not be returning these gifts.

We began to get letters which were mailed from different places without return address information. They were all threatening, hate letters from his mother. After seeing the content of the first couple, he threw the rest away unopened. She told him she disowned him and had disinherited him. His mother said he was *dead* to her. Knowing this was his maternal role model explained much of his unrealistic expectations of marriage.

Several years later, we received a call from her attorney saying that she had died. His mother had alienated her entire large family. The doctor and attorney were the only ones in attendance at her graveside service. This demented woman left her entire estate to her doctor. He declined taking it. The attorney wanted to send the money to us, but Bobby refused. He asked me what my favorite charity was. Bobby had it donated to the Paralyzed Vets. The attorney also said there was a box of family photos. He wanted to know if Bobby wanted them. Bobby was excited about this. "Maybe there is something good we can salvage here. I would love to have photos of my childhood and other family members." Bobby looked forward to the arrival of the box of photos.

I will never forget the day the box arrived. I came home to find Bobby sitting at the kitchen table. His head was in his hands and tears were streaming down his face. The pictures were all spread out. He had looked at each one. He said, "She curses me even in death." I then realized that his mother had carefully cut his head out of every single photograph. We never spoke of that day again, yet it was a turning point in our life. He was never the same. For a time, he began to drink more, and his insecurities became worse. He was angry and irrational, and he projected it onto me and the kids. The evil in her had found a new home. Try as he might to suppress it, we would all suffer because of her illness.

Our life was challenging enough, but for a time it came unhinged.

I believe mental illness is one of the most devastating and difficult conditions we can be faced with in this life. It is shocking what damage it can do. Families feel painfully powerless. I did my best to stay detached and observe the rippling effects of her insanity. I now clearly understood his unfinished family business. This is why he would project his mother-anger onto me. He had spent a lifetime trying desperately to be everything she was not.

CHAPTER 14

Pathways Manifested

Be still and know that I am God.

~Psalm 46:10

After a crises involving alcohol, Bobby stopped drinking. This was such a gift. He felt better and was more even tempered. These were a peaceful, harmonious few years. I became quite hopeful for our future. Life was manageable and fun again.

He had an uncanny way of playing me back to me, holding up the mirror. I was able to use this as a tool for my own growth in humility. I found the courage to change what I could which was myself. I realized, I was obsessing over the addicts in my life. I decided to take a positive step to deal with these feelings. I needed to learn some more effective ways of coping.

I spent a few years regularly participating in Al-Anon. I learned about the power of detachment and how to take responsibility for my own life. A wise woman once said her greatest fear was that her husband's life would pass before her eyes when she died. This described me perfectly. I became aware of how I spent much of my time taking inventories and micromanaging. I needed to resign as *general manager* of the universe. I was indeed powerless over other's lives. I only had power over my own life. I related to this definition of insanity: *Keep doing the same thing over and over again and expecting a different outcome.* I became aware of my own motives. Also, I learned to take responsibility and make amends for my own past and present destructive behaviors.

I began to understand that the spiritual path is really about doing your own ego work. By becoming more aware of this, I gained self-respect and thus recovered my self-esteem. This freed the people in my life to follow their own path. I was actually grateful to have addicted people in my life because it motivated me to find Al-Anon. With this Twelve Step program I experienced much growth and gained peace. The power of the group process is like experiencing a miracle every day of your life. It takes both courage and humility to become an honest, participating member of a support group. I found it well worth the effort.

I also joined *A Course in Miracles* study group. This was also about the ego. I learned to discern the difference between the voice of my ego and that of the *Divine* in me. One voice brings peace and the other brings turmoil. I became more aware of how judgmental I was, and that forgiveness was the key to healing the past. The group, which met weekly, was very powerful and the sharing was quite moving. I became close friends with two very special women, Marilee and Mukta. Through our group meditations, I experienced profound healing. I was taught how to set aside my ego in meditation and enter a state of receptive guidance from *Christ*. One day, I came home after meditating and Bobby asked me if I was having an affair. He said I seemed like a woman in love. I carefully explained to him that my energy field was vibrating much higher, and yes indeed, I was in a loving relationship with *Christ*.

I felt immensely blessed by the support and personal transformation I experienced from attending these gatherings of women. During this time, I found myself in a powerful kundalini dream: *A large snake entered my body at the base of my spine and exited through my crown.* I sat bolt right up in bed! My spiritual energy was further awakened.

In meditation, I was encouraged to find a way to connect with more women in order to teach and heal. I wanted to find a way to give something back to the community. I continued to have a deep interest in holistic medicine, (mind, body and spirit), all affecting our well-being. I was a voracious student of metaphysics.

Bobby and I were at a very healthy place in our marriage, as peaceful as was possible with his challenges. Even though it was his pattern to be quite controlling and possessive, we both came up with the idea of a bookstore at the same time. We had different motives, yet miraculously it worked. We rented a space and created a delightful atmosphere. There was a meeting room for classes and groups. My tagline was *Helping People Help Themselves.* We created an intimate bookstore with an array of books on various spiritual, religious, health, and psychological topics. I felt both driven and *Divinely* guided regarding this endeavor. The nurse in me saw it as a way to place myself in the community and allow *God* to do the rest. Bobby enjoyed the creative part of designing the business and healing center. He acted as a guard to protect the space which allowed the spiritual healing work to take place. He jokingly referred to himself as the *poster boy* for Pathways.

Bobby was always supportive of Pathways. It was as if a *Higher Force* was guiding him as well. He was never envious of my time or involvement. My new passion afforded me a break from our intense life together. I guess it gave him a break from me! I facilitated Twelve Step groups for everyone. No alcohol issues needed. We also held classes and women's circles. I brought in teachers from different backgrounds on a range of topics. A variety of clients, including professionals, found their way to Pathways over the years. Once again, I worked mostly with women. The exchange of ideas and the networking we provided was quite impactful. I always knew it was *God's* work The project lasted for five years.

I have a first cousin, Patrick, who I hadn't seen in many years. While visiting town, he strolled into Pathways one Saturday morning. I was both delighted and surprised. He was interested in getting to know me and my interests. As providence would have it, we had much in common. He is my kindred spirit as well as a powerful healer/teacher. His chiropractic practice focuses on holistic techniques. Through my networking, he was able to come to town on weekends to see patients. We quickly became close friends. Patrick has supported and mentored me through many difficult circumstances over the years. I am grateful for our special, committed, familial bond.

I had numerous interesting encounters with clients who visited my healing center. One individual I shall never forget. It was a bright, sunny, spring morning: A man of about twenty years of age, a pack on his back, wandered aimlessly into Pathways. Living in a college town, it was a natural assumption that he was a student. I was immediately struck by his eyes. They had a vacant look to them. He had a fierceness in his nature as he spoke. He wasted no time in striking up a conversation with me. He had glanced over the array of spiritual and holistic healing material on the bookshelves.

This intense guy started questioning me about whether I really believed what was written in them. There was a challenging tone to his inquiries. My intuition told me not to get involved in a verbal game of whose belief system is right or wrong. I turned the table and asked him what kinds of subjects *he* was interested in. The opinionated young man told me that he *definitely* did *not* believe in *God*. He was consumed by his delusional ideology and was on a quest to prove that there was no death. He believed he could overcome it and stay in this physical body forever. He got more and more excited as he spewed his beliefs to me. He seemed to have delusions of grandeur. I decided this was a good opportunity to engage in active listening. I merely mirrored his statements.

He said, "Yes, you do indeed hear me correctly." There was no death for him and this material world is *everything* and *all* that exists. He seemed so lost, alone, and sad yet so arrogant.

As he spoke, I began to have chills run up and down my spine. A voice inside me was struggling to get out. I knew immediately, this confused man was guided to this place and to me for a reason. I recognized this as an opportunity to plant a spiritual seed. I prayed to be used as *God's* instrument.

I said to him, in the most loving manner I could find in my heart: "You seem like such an intelligent guy. It is quite normal at your age to question every spiritual principal you have been exposed to. At one time, I did the very same thing. I would like to challenge you to try something. Would you be willing to take just five minutes a day to be perfectly still? Spend five minutes not talking or thinking, just listening to the beat and possibly the voice of your own heart? That is all I have to say about whether *God* exists. Perhaps you will find out for yourself." Interestingly enough, he said that he would consider doing this. He seemed intrigued by the challenge.

I soon dismissed the entire encounter. About two years later, I was facilitating a women's support group when I heard a knock at the door. I had since moved the location of my bookstore. There stood the same young man carrying the same back pack. He was unshaven and looked quite travel weary. He politely asked if he could speak to me for a moment. I excused myself from the group and stepped into the hallway. Missing, was the bravado in his voice that had been present in our previous encounter. I immediately noticed that his eyes were full of life, and he was grinning from ear to ear. His transformation was remarkable.

He said to me, "I have hitch-hiked all over the United States since I saw you last. I have never forgotten our encounter. I traveled a hundred miles out of my way to find you again. I wanted to tell you that I took your challenge. I spent those five minutes a day *listening* and guess what? You were so right. *God* does exist. In those five minutes a day, I found my *true self* and my connection to *God*. I will always be grateful to you for taking the time and caring enough to challenge my thinking. I now have peace. I came to thank you." I spontaneously hugged him.

With that he was gone, and I never saw him again. I will never forget our conversation. I have often found that taking risks, when your motive is love, can and does create fertile soil for miracles. Do what you can and get out of the way. Let *God* do the rest. A spiritual awakening is a wonder to behold.

During these Pathways years, I was very aware of my dreams. I was constantly being guided, working out my inner spiritual life. I dreamt: *I was climbing a very steep cliff. It was an arduous journey. It was all I could do to secure my footing and keep moving upward. Just as the trek became impossible, I realized there was someone climbing ahead of me. This climber reached down and took my hand to pull me up. I was amazed, relieved, and very grateful. I then looked behind me to see that there was an infinite number of climbers behind me. I reached down to help the next person and on it went. The line ahead came into view, and all the climbers were assisting each other. Eventually, I was assisted to the top of the mountain. The scenery was spectacular, more beautiful than I could ever imagine! I realized this is how we are to keep reaching new heights in our evolution ... certain we are never climbing alone.*

Another very special experience involved an older lady who was guided to me. I'll call her Alice. She was a survivor of the holocaust and had endured much trauma in the concentration camps. There was a fierceness and strength of character about her. Alice shared her personal story of years of physical disability and pain due to crippling arthritis. She became aware that the anger she was holding onto was destroying her body. She spent many hours in bed, near death, wrestling with her ego. During this episode, she was able to release the past through forgiveness. It was a transformative, spiritual experience for her. Her act of forgiveness left her healed and free from pain. Her hands were crippled from the disease, but she no longer had pain.

As her life unfolded, Alice met Judy who was an extremely intelligent professional on a spiritual path. Judy was proficient at meditating and also a gifted intuitive and medium. This special lady had begun to channel a spirit by the name of Red Hawk. This happened quite spontaneously when she was in trance. She did readings, by referral only, when she was passing through town. Alice asked me if I would be interested in a session? I was quite curious and met with her. I did believe in mediums and channels but had never experienced it for myself.

I met with her for a private session. Judy went into a deep trance and her body posture, voice, and face, changed. I felt like I was sitting at the foot of a spiritual master. In this case, a *medicine man*. Her voice transformed into masculine as well. Red Hawk asked what I wanted from him. Knowing this was possible, I asked if James had any messages for me.

He said, "James is present, and he wants you to know he loves you more now than when he was in body with you." I was shocked because this is exactly what I had been saying since he died. I loved him more now than when he was here on the earth with

me. Then Red Hawk said, "He is troubled that you are holding a grievance over something. He is asking that you forgive him and release it."

I immediately knew he was referring to the pregnancy termination. I agreed to let it go, and I told him I loved him. There were other messages regarding people in my life. Each one was helpful and insightful. The entire experience was meaningful, and I believe quite authentic.

I met many psychotherapists at Pathways. They would come in to peruse the library of interesting books. I facilitated a closed Twelve Step group for professionals. Many lives were enriched due to the power of the group process. I worked with teenagers teaching them recovery principals. Therapists in the community referred their clients my way. During this period, I was in meditation and *Jesus came to me. He* said, *"I will guide you."* Each day brought spiritual surprises.

I share these stories because they illustrate the unseen forces that influence our lives. When I remember to ask for support, it has always been there. I witnessed the hand of the *Divine* at work with many clients in spiritual crises. Pathways was a humbling and rewarding chapter in my life. I was able to practice getting out of the way and allowing God to lead the way. I was privileged to experience synchronicity at work on a daily basis.

CHAPTER 15

A Forever Love

You don't really understand something unless you
can explain it to your grandmother.

~Albert Einstein

My grandmother was a formidable woman. A devout Christian, she took pride in living up to her interpretation of what that meant. She was loyal to her friends, loved ones, and had a powerful dedication to her grandchildren. My mother and I lived with my grandparents my first year of life and on the same ranch for the next eight years. We became extremely close. She was the type of mentor who taught you about life by allowing you to practice. That meant you could cut and perm her hair, clean her house, arrange her furniture, cook in her kitchen (as long as you cleaned up the mess), camp with her, travel with her, sleep with her, try anything you wanted to learn. Let us not forget the funeral experiences!

She had a wonderful sense of humor and was the original *general manager* of the universe. She single-handedly kept an inventory of the lives of each and every member of the family. Often, my grandmother did not know where she ended and the rest of us began.

We remained very close over her lifetime. She was always available to support me through the ups and downs of life. We resided in the same town for the last several years of her life. Being the nurse in the family, I was the obvious one to look after her myriad medical problems; doctor appointments, surgeries, and much of her day to day requests and needs. In fact, the entire family did their best to rally around her.

Grandma often expressed to me, "I feel closest to *God* when I am in the mountains." I too experienced this same awareness. One morning, at our mountain hideaway, I had another out-of-body experience. I was napping on a recliner on the quiet back deck. The sun was streaming all around me. I heard the birds singing and the scurrying chipmunks in the trees. I suddenly found myself out of my body. The sensation was pure and perfect energetic harmony. I was startled and quickly popped back into my body. I perceived my intimate connection to the *Divine*. It was glorious!

Bobby and I spent much quality time with my grandmother. She was fascinated with him. He was incredibly generous and kind to her. They loved to tease each other. Many humorous stories were often shared. The holidays were always more special because of their childlike love of them. She represented the extended family he didn't have. I believe in her heart, she recognized his soul's beauty and need for acceptance.

Grandma would often ask me to take her to the cemetery to put flowers on my grandfather's grave.

The ritual was always the same on these outings. She would tell him that she loved him and would cry. She'd tell me that she assumed none of the family would come to put flowers on their graves after she died. It just wasn't a priority to the younger generations. I constantly reassured her that I would faithfully visit their graves after she left this earth. Year after year, we had the identical conversation.

In the spring of her eighty-fifth year, I had a dream: *There was a large circle of people sitting cross legged on the ground. I looked directly across the circle from me and there sat my grandmother. She was radiant and smiling and obviously very happy. In the center of the circle was baby **Jesus** in a manger.*

Upon awakening from the dream, I knew in my heart I was being forewarned of her upcoming death. I assumed this was a gift, and it afforded me time to have closure with her. I did heed the dream. I began having more intimate conversations with her regarding our life together, my appreciation of her, and the important role she played in my life. I wanted her to know just how much I deeply loved her. I also made certain that whenever I was in her presence, I gave her my undivided attention. I practiced being totally present in each moment. The other topic we discussed was communicating with each other after her death. I told her if she could come to me … I would listen for her. She promised she would try.

Nine months later, she was admitted to a nursing home after a brief hospitalization. She always said these were places you go to die. For two days, she kept telling me that her head was itching. She even wanted a brush to scratch it. I had read this can be a sign of the crown chakra opening and getting ready for the spirit to exit the body. The next day, she was admitted to the hospital with a possible bowel obstruction.

I sat at her bedside and gave her light massages which she loved. I noticed she was confused between hot and cold which is also another possible sign of impending death. The next evening, after we had been visiting, I tucked her in. We exchanged our love. Immediately upon arriving home, the hospital called saying she was dying. We rushed back to her room. By then, she had transitioned. The rest of the family arrived, and we comforted each other briefly. We stroked her and cried. Soon after this, we left as it was very late.

There seemed to be no reason to linger now that she was gone. Bobby was extremely distraught. He stood in the hospital corridor and sobbed. I did my best to comfort him. She frequently would say, "I don't care what anyone says, I like Bob." He would miss that love and acceptance.

Three days later, I woke up in the morning and felt her standing by my bed. I could hear her voice in my mind. She admonished me quite sternly:

"Sherry, don't ever leave the bedside of a recently departed loved one ... so soon. I didn't even know I was dead! It was quite distressing to have witnessed all that was going on and the immediate removal of my body. You need to sit with the body and talk to the loved one. Tell them they have died and reassure them."

This was all there was to the message. I told her I got the message loud and clear! I had a chuckle realizing she was still teaching me.

I spoke at her open casket funeral. And yes, she was dressed in her finest fancy clothes complete with a perfumed hanky. It took strength for me to pull it off. I believed it would make her happy. I wanted it to be a service that was personally honoring of her life. On a chair next to the casket was a stuffed bear my daughter had given her. There was a balloon tied to it. During my eulogy, the bear jumped off the stool! After the service, we let eighty-six balloons fly. As they ascended and before they separated, the initial of her first name formed. She let us know she was still with us.

Later that year, I woke up one morning and there she was speaking in my inner ear once again: *"Sherry, it's my birthday, and I want flowers on my grave!"*

I jumped out of bed and went to the calendar. It most certainly was her birthday. As you can imagine, I saw to it there was a beautiful bouquet placed on my grandparent's grave that day.

From time to time, she continues to visit me in my dreams. It is usually preceding some difficult challenge I am about to face. Her dedicated presence in my life taught me at a young age that love had many faces; loyalty, honesty, joy, mentoring, and unconditional love of family. Her dedication has *undeniably* survived her death.

CHAPTER 16

Endurance Tested

When you have exhausted all possibilities, remember this: you haven't.

~Thomas Edison

Following my grandmother's death, Bobby and I enjoyed another short cycle of relative peace and happiness. I was, once again, being lulled into a sense of trust. There was so much appreciation for our life and all that was good. Bobby continued to wake up every morning with pure passion for life. We encouraged the kids to be grateful for their blessings.

Bobby told me that he hoped all the special, thoughtful things he did would somehow make up for his dark side. If only it were that simple. When I was totally unprepared, another crisis erupted. I realized his primary experience in therapy was to try and understand the behavior and motives of the people in his life. He never examined his own shadow. This projection is a common borderline trait.

Bobby had started to socially drink again. He was under the influence on this particular occasion. We purchased a collectible lamp at the flea market. He was excited to hang it on the patio. As always, I was his right-hand man in projects. I dreaded these times because his expectations were so high. I was perched on a stool and lost my balance. I dropped my end of the fixture. As a result, a corner chipped off. Being such a perfectionist, he was furious. I apologized profusely but to no avail. The lamp was usable, yet it would never be perfect again. It's a material thing. How important can this be? The harder I tried to reassure him, the more agitated and angry he became. I could see he was no longer able to reason.

I went in the kitchen hoping he would calm himself. No such luck. He followed me yelling, cursing, and verbally abusing me. He was so full of unbridled emotions. I was overwhelmed by the intensity of the situation. His diatribe continued to escalate. Out of desperation I asked, "What are you, crazy?" My question only served to escalate the situation. This was a poor decision on my part was. The one thing he feared most in life was following in his mother's footsteps. I had pulled the hidden trigger that unlocked his fear and rage. All sensibility vanished.

He reached back with a closed fist and hit me on the chin. I was totally in shock. The moment he hurt me, he crumpled to the floor. He was more devastated than I was. I have never seen such fear and sorrow. I realized that I needed to get out of the situation. He said, "You should leave. Pack your bags and leave right now."

I ran out the front door and was sobbing hysterically. I had just experienced my worst fear. I sat down on the curb in front of the house of all places. I calmed myself and took my physical inventory. I was shaking uncontrollably, but I was going to be fine. My ego was bruised much worse than my body. I quickly assessed that this had been an isolated circumstance preceded by a perfect storm. He had no pattern of physical abuse. He had used his fists for survival in New York, however, he prided himself on being in control of this once needed survival tool. His moral compass and Catholic guilt always held him back if he was on the verge of going too far. He could not tolerate anyone coloring outside the lines, especially when it was him. I believe that is why he dissociated at these times, which left him with amnesia.

I thought about all of the abused women I had cared for. How many of them had been in this exact circumstance? I had been judgmental, often believing I knew the answer to their dilemma. I had broken my promise to myself to never provoke him. The kids were smart enough not to cross that line.

I was confused because this had happened during a time when we were very happy as a family. I didn't know this is classic borderline behavior. I sat on that curb and prayed. I asked *Jesus* what he would do? I fully realized I had options. Through my internal clairaudience, I received a clear answer, "***The choice is yours. Remember, I am your guiding light.***" I felt shaken but at peace.

I went back into the house and surveyed the damage to my face. Miraculously, I only had a tiny bruise on my chin. He must have hit me at the strongest part of my jaw. Bobby was totally calm now. He asked me what I was going to do? I told him I did not intend to live in fear of him. In order for me to stay, he would have to promise to never physically hurt me again. If that meant therapy or whatever was necessary to deal with his shadow, then so be it. I feared he had dissociated and would not remember the incident. I calmly assured him, "This is the first and the last time I will forgive this. If you ever threaten me physically again, I will divorce you no matter the cost or difficulty. I love me enough to move on."

In that moment, I once again became the perfect enabler and secret keeper. I had set a boundary, but how would I live up to it? We had moved to another level of dysfunction. I had gone down the rabbit hole with him. I realized it was the beginning of the end of the marriage for me. All the love in the world was not going to fix this man. For me, trust was destroyed. I knew I had to save myself. I decided to wait and listen for *God* to guide me. In my biological family, the opposite of everything was true. Secret keeping became part of our normal life. With Bobby, the passion and dysfunction were usually on full display. With no witnesses, I was free to decide my fate. I felt deep shame about this traumatic event.

Chaos was honing my personality. In the face of adversity, I was given the opportunity to truly discover my strengths. It took complete focus to face and embrace life and to continue to find meaning. This was in spite of the overwhelming emotion which followed this episode.

My love and belief in family is what kept me going. Miraculously, our children were thriving and successful on all fronts. I was certain they had gone underground with their concerns. Life for a child with a parent who is so perfectionistic and unpredictable became increasingly more difficult as the years rolled on. I found myself often in the middle defending the children to him. Amazingly, the kids had enough self-esteem and strong foundation of love to withstand the traumas of our family life.

The hardest part for me was Bobby's denial of his own problems. I was continually trying to enlighten him about normal childhood behavior. He was guilty of caring too much and over-parenting. This created distrust in Alysia and over the years she withdrew from him more and more. As the kids grew into their teens, it triggered his abandonment issues. A struggle of their wills ensued. I did my best to keep peace and understanding between us. From my perspective, Sam had the advantage of early bonding with his dad. His relationship was less complicated.

I had been having numerous dreams with death symbols in them. They always involved Bobby and his recklessness. In one dream: *I was standing on a newly poured grave marker and I saw a name emerging. It was my married name.* Deep in my soul, I knew transformative change was on the horizon. He lived life with such abandon. His health habits followed the same pattern as so many of his other choices. Although he had quit smoking, he continued to be bulimic and abuse alcohol on a regular basis. I dreamt of cemeteries, headstones, and caskets. I felt I was being prepared for some new challenge. One of my friends dreamt *I was living in a web ... totally trapped.* Even so, laughter was the daily remedy which eased our pain. We had this uncanny ability to step back and see humor most days as if we were living out a great cosmic joke.

As time went on, we were in an escalating emotional family dynamic. I went to therapy to discuss my concerns for my family. I did not confess that he had hit me. I had convinced myself that it had been an isolated instance and I did not want it to become the focus of our life. This was classic dysfunction, and I knew it. Bobby's dissociative episodes were more frequent. He was becoming verbally abusive to everyone he loved. His moods would shift dramatically without warning. He was fiercely controlling, insecure, and angry. His outbursts started taking a toll on the kids as well. They had nothing more to look forward to than hours and hours of lecturing and ranting. During these times, none of us were allowed to speak only listen.

I knew he was mentally sick. He needed to be on medication. I tried to explain to the kids that he was not in control of his behaviors. I emphasized repeatedly that this was not their fault. We all dreaded being in his presence. I kept trying to be tolerant and loving while at the same time taking care of my own emotional needs. More and more, I turned to my friends for support. I had long ago lost the desire to put on a front for anyone. Our life was spinning out of control. During one of his paranoid episodes, he decided I had betrayed him by discussing his drinking with a friend. From that day forward, he was angry with me and shut me out emotionally. We were fourteen years into our relationship.

He didn't feel well physically. I once found him lying on the bed in the middle of the day and he said to me, "I just want to die. I feel so horrible." I wondered if he was just being his usual theatrical self because he had no specific symptoms to report. I offered to get him a doctor's appointment. He declined.

I began to notice a small mass on his neck. At first, I assumed it was a swollen gland from the bulimia. His glands were often quite swollen. He was quite fearful about his health, and I did not like to alarm him. Finally, one day he felt the lump himself. He said, "What the hell is this?" I examined it thoroughly and realized it was an enlarging hard mass. I instinctively knew it was cancer but didn't say so. I told him we needed to get a doctor's opinion.

I scheduled him with a wonderful ear-nose-throat (ENT) doctor who I knew in the next town. He was Italian. I thought he and Bobby would get along famously, and they did. The doctor tried antibiotics for a couple of weeks with no results. The mass was growing quite rapidly now. This was followed by a needle biopsy. I remember the exact moment the phone call came with the results.

The Italian doctor said, "I am sorry to give you this news. You have cancer. This is a metastatic tumor on your neck. We will do more tests to see where the primary tumor is." The doctor scheduled a CAT scan which revealed a large primary mass in the base of Bobby's tongue. Our life now became all about cancer. The shocking news brought us to our knees and created a sobering new reality for our family.

I wept for my husband, for our children, and for myself. My nerves were frayed from all of the emotional turmoil of the year leading up to the cancer discovery. I knew at some deep level this illness was affecting his psyche, and that his escalating emotional behavior was a resulting symptom. He was strangely calm about it at first. I think he was in shock. The biopsy showed stage four squamous cell carcinoma. I did my own research and learned that the five-year survival rate for this type of cancer was only fifteen percent.

The doctor told us it was very serious. Because of Bobby's age, fifty-one, he wanted him to go to the University of California San Francisco for a consult.

He felt the university setting had the most to offer us. We scheduled the appointment. The following week, we took all of our test results to San Francisco. We met with the leading specialist. He put Bobby's CAT scan up to the light to examine it. He palpated the mass on his neck and looked at his throat. It was the first time I had seen the large lump in his throat on film. The doctor then shook his head and said, "Too bad *God* chose you for this type of cancer." I couldn't believe my ears! What kind of a thing is that to say to a patient? I couldn't imagine words that would invoke any more fear. He wanted us to see the tumor board that very day.

We waited several hours, and a host of doctors re-examined him. They met as a group to discuss their findings. They then met with us to give their recommendations. The doctors told us there was a chance for a cure if they brought out all the *big guns*. This would involve a three-part treatment plan. There would be six weeks of external beam radiation to the neck and jaw area. This would take place close to home. We would go back to UCSF for another radiation procedure. This would involve putting several catheters into the tumor at the base of the tongue followed by more radiation sent through these catheters, requiring a week in the hospital. Following this stage, a major surgical procedure would be performed to remove the lump on his neck and all the lymph nodes surrounding it. They would also be removing much of neck tissue. The entire treatment plan would take three months.

I asked what would happen if he chose to have no treatment. I knew we needed to know all of his options. Clearly, the treatment was going to be torturous with little chance of a remission. They explained that without treatment his throat would close up from the tumor. His airway would be cut off. He would die a slow and painful death with a feeding tube and tracheotomy to breathe. This news certainly pushed us in the direction of treatment. We asked what would happen if the treatment didn't work? What was the next step?

The physician said, "You would require removal of the tongue." This news was horrifying to say the least. This fast-talking Italian, whose life was all about verbalizing, was devastated at the thought of what might lie ahead.

Being a nurse, I knew we were about to face the challenge of a lifetime. The emotional roller coaster we had lived on for so many years was now going to take a trip through hell. I knew he was tough, but I had no idea if he had the emotional strength for the journey. I was certain it was going to take a toll on all of us. I think the kids were in shock during most of this. They observed everything that was happening to him. They were teenagers and quite busy with their own lives. Mercifully, this afforded them constant distractions. Sam and Alysia tried to be emotionally supportive to him in spite of his high expectations of them.

Bobby got a lot of mileage out of this cancer diagnosis. Living in a small town, it didn't take long for the word to spread. I found that most people are at a total loss as to what to do at a time like this. My immediate family was tremendously empathetic, but Bobby pushed them away. My close friends were there for me, yet what could they do besides listen?

He told everyone he was dying. We received plenty of upgraded tables in restaurants and accommodations in hotels. He shouted it from the rooftops. I thought, "What if he doesn't die?" He sold his private collections of antique toys and started making plans to die. I encouraged him to be hopeful and to send *live* messages to his cells. I urged him to make peace with his life and to forgive. He was angry and demanding.

Most of his friends fell by the wayside. Thankfully, there was one friend who came every week, without fail, to visit him. This wonderful man had so much empathy for us. Mike witnessed some pretty scary things over those months. He continued to come and just sit and listen to Bobby rant on and on for hours. He was definitely Bobby's angel.

The treatment was gruesome. By that, I mean absolutely inhumane. I personally could not survive it. He was physically tough, so very tough. He told me, "I consider myself rugged, but this has really got my attention." He lost forty pounds. I looked inside his mouth and there was raw burned tissue from his lips all the way down his throat. I burst into tears when I saw it. Every swallow was an excruciating experience which brought tears. The mucous drained from the burns, and he would choke on it at night. The stench from the burned and rotting tissue in his throat was grotesque. I felt so sorry for him. I began another performance of putting on a confident front. I tried to convince him that I was okay and so was he, and we would get through this. I was at his side day and night. I made blender drinks of high protein content and fed him round the clock like an infant. It would be a year before he could learn to eat again. I would put the drinks on ice at his bedside. He called it his *team*. We kept him alive this way, and eventually he even gained weight on the drinks.

The doctors said he had the worst case of mucositis they had ever seen. The good news was that the tumor on his neck shrunk rapidly from the external beam radiation. The radiologist told us he would never be able to have any dental work because of the radiation. They were giving him the maximum dose these tissues could have over a lifetime. He begged the doctors to stop the radiation early because the pain was so extreme. They insisted that the dosages had been carefully measured and were necessary. He reluctantly finished the treatment.

Following this, we had a break for a few weeks. Just when he was just starting to feel somewhat better it was time to go to UCSF for round two. By now, he was a totally crazed man mentally. The stress of the treatment and of thinking about his condition brought to the surface the worst of his personality disorder symptoms. There was no longer any alcohol in his life or food for that matter. He found it difficult to talk through the copious mucous drainage. He continually spit it out. Believe it or not, talking was his only distraction. He never stopped yelling and cussing at us. The verbal abuse was incessant. When it was time to go to UCSF, he told me he hated me. He wanted me out of his life, and he definitely didn't want me to go to the hospital with him. I knew he wasn't in his right mind. I kindly informed him that I was going. That was all there was to it. He yelled at me the entire two-hour drive to San Francisco.

When we arrived, they started the unbelievable process of taking him down further. Doctors surgically implanted twelve plastic catheters through the underside of his chin into the base of his tongue. They catheterized his bladder, put a feeding tube in his stomach, and started an intravenous solution. Nurses put motorized leg apparatus on to keep his legs pumping blood. He was to lie flat on his back for seven days and *not* talk. The panic in his eyes was that of a frightened helpless creature. He wrote notes on a clipboard. The harder I tried to guess what he was trying to say, the more frustrated he would become. One night, he threw the board across the room in desperation and anger. He found ways to verbally abuse me without speaking!

One night, I let down. I remember standing in the hallway outside his room crying. I think I had held my breath the entire week. It felt liberating to release my pent-up emotions. There was a sweet nurse who found me there. She hugged me and conveyed her true empathy for my situation. I asked the doctor to give Bobby some sort of sedation. They put him on Compazine for the nausea. The drug seemed to calm him down. With this leg of the treatment almost behind him, he turned a corner. He thanked me for coming and being there for him. He had no memory of his earlier outbursts. This was his pattern. He was always so gentle and appreciative after a dissociative episode.

As a reward for this week from hell, the mucositis and throat ulcerations began again. He wasn't healed from this round of radiation before he was scheduled for the radical neck surgery. The term *radical* was an understatement.

In San Francisco I had a hotel room. I gratefully retreated to my cozy room about midnight daily. This saved my life. I stayed in the hospital round the clock during all of his other procedures. I would inform the staff that I was a nurse. I'd ask where the linen and supplies were, and I would take care of him.

The surgery caused tremendous swelling of his face and neck. Again, the pain was incredible. The good news was that there was no cancer left in the now small lump they removed from his neck. The surgery was actually not even needed. It left him with what he called a pencil neck. He would have a lifetime of little or no saliva production and no sense of taste.

I often thought if all smokers could witness this perhaps quitting would be easier for them. This was believed to be a smoking related cancer. From the day he was diagnosed, he was never bulimic again nor did he ever have another glass of wine. Red wine was his favorite alcoholic beverage. Eventually, he was able to drink beer, Corona Light being his choice. He was required to have checkups every three months to examine the tissues for any recurrence. He told me he had asked *God* to let him live long enough to finish raising Sam. He was in a total remission, and this felt like a miracle.

His day to day existence was miserable at first. He could not raise his left arm from the neck surgery. I scheduled him for massage therapy which, over time, allowed him to golf again. When the prescription for Compazine ran out, he was back to the angry demanding and controlling personality.

What do you do with a sick and suffering soul? You put one foot in front of the other and care for them. You take care of yourself the best you can. I knew I was the glue that held the family together. I lived one day at a time. I affirmed my strength daily. My close friend Terrie, said to me, "You must be in this relationship to learn endurance." This was an epiphany for me. I knew she spoke the truth.

It actually was a tremendous help to think of this chapter of my life as an opportunity to develop a spiritual quality. I surmised, "I only learn endurance if I keep pushing forward." I wasn't finished. There is beauty in every day. I slowed down and looked for it.

Golf was his personal passion. We decided to move to a golfing community in the Palm Springs area. This was his dream. He was a big city boy in a small town. He had felt out of his element for years. One day he said, "What are you going to do … scatter my ashes over the fairgrounds? *I don't want to die here*."

I somehow found the strength to sell the house and most of our possessions. We bought a furnished condominium in a lovely gated golfing resort. A new life was waiting for us. Sam had one more year in high school, and he decided to live with us full time. Alysia had just graduated from college and took a sabbatical to teach and make her choice for graduate school. The cancer remained in remission. Our entire family was optimistic about starting over. I was committed to focusing on all that was good in our life and begin again.

CHAPTER 17

Instability Resurfaces

If nothing ever changed there'd be no butterflies.

~Unknown

In the beginning, our new life in the desert was fun and exciting. The fresh new environment renewed our confidence in the joys of family life and our marriage. Unfortunately, the cloud of apprehension and worry over the cancer returning was always playing in the background.

Bobby continued to have regular checkups to keep a watch for any signs of cancer recurrence. These visits only involved palpation and inspection of the throat which remained negative. Each visit brought up the same tension and fear. Bobby's frustration and anger would surface for a couple of weeks. We would ride out the emotional storms we had grown so accustomed to, and slowly life would return to a familiar rhythm. It has been said that adversity introduces you to yourself. He went from being his best self to his worst self during each cycle. I merely hung on for dear life.

We existed in this difficult, yet hopeful, state for a couple of years. We did our best to build a new life. After a year of teaching, Alysia went to San Diego to continue her educational pursuit of obtaining a doctoral degree. Bobby's abandonment issues were deeply triggered by the advancing age and independence of the kids. Over time, he began to get more and more irrational and combative. These episodes could occur with little or no provocation. The arguments between us become more volatile. I was so disappointed and resentful, and I found myself running out of patience. We respected his delicate emotional state. I had truly allowed myself to believe that things could be different in this new environment. I had always believed his acting out was an immature type of begging for love.

It began to be harder and harder to stay in a loving compassionate space. I was aware of the futility in believing there would ever be a change in his temperament. I longed for the early days of our marriage. What happened to the Pathways chapter? Life had been at times difficult, but mostly manageable in the early years of our marriage.

I dreamt I was running around the same track, and the dirt was becoming quicksand. I also dreamt I was in jail.

I reminded myself that deep in his soul he wanted happiness. I was so confused. It began to feel like I was living a lie, always putting on a happy face armored for the next barrage of insults. I was overwhelmed much of the time. The levity that we relied upon to smooth out the jagged edges of our relationship had vanished. Strangers would stop me and ask with concern about his inappropriate behavior. I donned my poker face and assured them that I was fine.

In his desperation to control me, the verbal assaults became more personal. I was confused, not by his words, but from his need to hurt me in this way. This destroyed the trust that had been painstakingly built over and over again. How many times could the phoenix rise from the ashes? It was as if his coping skills were non-existent. He had lost all ability to give or receive love. No manner of boundary setting was effective. Each attempt only served to escalate the crises. He was a master at deflection.

Our life had once again spun out of control. Bobby knew he had lost my trust. He could no longer keep his inner monsters in check. The intimate pillow talks we once relied on nightly, as a safe place to process our life, had disappeared. Gone was the childlike enthusiasm and pride he once felt for his family. He was clearly out of touch with reality. He was circling the drain and taking me and the kids with him. We were two souls living one life, and that is dysfunction and codependency at its peak.

As the emotional outbursts accelerated, the kids and I joined forces doing our best to understand the situation. We focused on taking care of ourselves and each other. I knew something in his brain had changed. I did not understand. My good friend, Susan, said, "Maybe he's getting ready to die."

Eventually, I came to believe that he was subconsciously pushing us away in preparation for the end. His fear of death was too difficult for him to face. Sabotage was the path of least resistance for him. I had experienced versions of this behavior over our time together, but this was different. His appetite for total control was consuming us. I now believe this was in direct proportion to the rapidly advancing disease spreading through his body and brain.

I know that life is like a roller coaster ride. When you are going down it is as if all is lost, but if you hang on the ride always goes back up again. This was my day to day existence. He justified his projected fear and anger. I took the brunt of it because the kids had their own lives to live. Bobby was my life. Now that I had moved away from my family and friends, I was even more immersed in the codependent cycle. The relationship was torched and in a state of meltdown if I made even the slightest move to defend myself, the kids, or others. I reached out to my closest confidants by email and telephone. The support I received helped to sustain me.

One very intuitive friend cautioned me strongly, "He may become physically abusive." I didn't want to believe that. The verbal assaults were quite enough. I knew all too well that what she warned could happen. One day it did. He was being extremely caustic and cruel. I set a boundary, and this angered him further. He grabbed me by the throat and pinned me against the wall with his fist raised, threatening to hit me. I very calmly and firmly ordered him to put me down. The evil in his eyes dissipated, and he released me. Where was the love?

The time had come to love myself in a healthier way. As my friend put it, "Walk out with your head held high." I read a book about the dilemma of making a decision to leave or stay when so much of your life seems good, yet there is also a recurring dysfunctional pattern. When I came to the chapter on respect, I had the answer I was seeking. I deserved the respect I had always given. It was unacceptable for me to have any less than that. My decision to love him had always felt like a *soul assignment*. Now what?

I told him that I was now prepared to keep my promise to myself. If he ever got physical with me again that I would be forced to leave. That time had arrived. He was flabbergasted. "When have I ever been physically abusive to you?" He truly had no memory of even the recent past. This confirmed once again that he dissociated at these times.

I sat him down and firmly told him, "I have loved you beyond measure. I deserve to be treated with respect *all of the time*." It had become abundantly clear that he no longer had the desire or the ability.

He hung his head in shame and said, "You are absolutely correct. You don't deserve this, and I understand. If I ever do it again, just leave and don't look back." I knew he couldn't keep any promises he would make. He now realized that, emotionally, I had already left the relationship. I was finally being totally authentic, and he did not have to like it! The hardest type of love to give is the pulling back kind. It is loving enough to let go.

Following this conversation, an interesting thing happened. He laid on our bed and curled up in a fetal position. He began to sweat and shake uncontrollably. He was violently ill. It was if a powerful internal battle was being raged deep inside of him. I instinctively crawled into bed and held him from behind. I cradled him in my arms while his body shuddered and convulsed for several minutes. When the symptoms subsided, I went into the guest room and slept a deep peaceful sleep. I had at last told the entire truth. I put my life in *God's* hands. Once again, I prayed for guidance.

The following day found us both in a peaceful and loving state. I felt calm knowing my cards were all on the table. Bobby seemed at peace realizing that he had faced his own demons the night before. We never discussed that night again. There was a new harmony in our life for the next month. The laughter and goodwill were back. I knew some sort of healing had happened for both of us. Perhaps we had each harnessed our own egos. I did not know what would happen within our relationship, but it no longer seemed to matter. The particulars would be worked out soon. I was starting to envision myself in a new life without him.

I never lost sight of the fact that our time together was mostly full of happiness and meaning. I stayed for all those years because I believed in commitment, family, love, and that our relationship had a karmic lesson. I believe that breaking up a family is the absolute last resort. We were together for a *higher purpose* and we couldn't fulfill it if we walked away. The dark cloud that had grown in power over the years was threatening to destroy everything now.

The taking back of my power and loving myself was an important lesson for me. I was experiencing the courage and humility that it takes to accomplish this feat. I dreamt *I had been let out of jail*. I also had a dream that *I was awarded a PhD*. I can tell you I earned one!

A few days later, Bobby had been out hitting golf balls on the driving range when he became very short of breath. He came home to lie down. I took his blood pressure, and it was erratic. I thought he might be having a heart attack, and I urged him to let me take him to the hospital. He refused. He lay in bed for a couple of days with a heavy chest and labored breathing. I began calling for a doctor. When I described his symptoms, I was told to take him to an emergency room. After much pleading, he finally consented. Upon arriving at the hospital, they immediately took a CAT scan and found fluid around his heart and in his lungs. The doctors insisted on doing several tests plus a trip to surgery to do a biopsy and remove the fluid.

The next day, he felt much better. The pressure had been removed from his chest. I was sitting at his bedside when a doctor came in the room. He introduced himself and without making eye contact he said, "You have cancer in the pericardium, the sack surrounding your heart. We will start chemotherapy tomorrow. It is not the same type of cancer cell that you had the first time. This is new, and we don't know where the original tumor is. It doesn't matter because if we don't get this treated you will die." With that he vanished as quickly as he had come. We were both in shock. Without warning, this man we had never met comes in and drops this bomb! Being a nurse, I was infuriated with the lack of compassion and communication skills of this doctor.

Naturally, Bobby was devastated. We just sat there in shock as his fear filled the room. I knew he was very frightened of chemotherapy. We had been so relieved that he didn't have any chemo with the first cancer. The radiation side effects were devastating enough. He was still living with the aftermath. It had been three and half years since the first cancer. I said to him, "You are in charge of your body. This doctor is not. We can get a second opinion. You do not have to start chemotherapy tomorrow." He was relieved and humbly asked me to line it up for him. I did exactly what I promised.

The following day, a different physician arrived. She was much more compassionate and explained the situation quite thoroughly including all of our options.

We did more tests. None of them showed where the primary tumor was located, nor did they show any masses anywhere in the body. The final test, called a PET scan, revealed malignant nodes all over the lungs, intestines, and adrenal glands. I often wondered if the cancer filling his adrenal glands had something to do with his erratic temperament. At any rate, sadly, there was cancer all over his body.

We met with the oncologist again. She was very direct as she kindly said, "There is no cure for the cancer. Chemotherapy is the only option. The chemotherapy, if it is effective, may buy you some extra time. The side effects will be severe. The other option is to treat the symptoms of your cancer as they arise. You can live out your life without heroic measures."

Bobby said, "Death is going to have to come and get me on the golf course. I am not going to spend what time I have left being pumped full of chemicals." I admired his courage and his choice. I talked with several doctors regarding his decision. They all agreed that if it were them, they would choose palliative care.

When all the information was assimilated, I concluded that the bazaar, out of control, behavior he was demonstrating was a result of his body being full of cancer. Now that the mystery was solved, we would do our best to live out the terminal diagnosis. He said to me, "Let's end this well." Since his pattern was to incite constant chaos, I knew this was going to be the ultimate challenge for him. We both were aware he was referring to the place we had reached in our relationship. I agreed with him and recommitted to the marriage. With Bobby by my side, I would see it through to the end. I was being true to what I had originally promised, *until death do us part.* I prepared myself for the last chapter.

CHAPTER 18

Facing the End

To die will be an awfully big adventure.

~Peter Pan

As I began to look at my own behaviors and motives, I was able to become more detached. I became an observer of my own life which allowed me to live in the present moment. This was a much healthier mental state, and I felt less vulnerable … free from fear. I prayed for the strength and courage to know my role in assisting the highest outcome possible in our situation.

Much like you look at the face of the flight attendant when the ride gets bumpy, I knew that once again Bobby would look to me to see if he were alright. Thus, began the third acting performance of my life. I did not want him to live out his days in fear. If I showed distress, it would no doubt have a snowball effect on the family. I was so exhausted from the months of emotional turmoil and it was incredibly painful to watch him face the end of his passionate life. With fortitude, I rallied. He made me promise that I would not cry in front of him. I agreed to do my best. I did not want to make his dying any more miserable than it already was.

I expressed to Bobby, "You are a true sage. I am smarter, stronger, deeper, and more evolved spiritually for having known you so intimately." I told him he had demonstrated great courage and endurance. I thanked him for holding a vision of greater things for all of us even in our darkest hours. I reminded him of his dedication as a father, serving his children before himself. The one quality I valued the most was his ability to turn any situation into humor. He could hold up the mirror and allow me to look at my own shadow. I gave thanks for all that was good in our healthier years. This was closure for me. I wanted to squeeze every ounce of growth and spiritual understanding out of this life as was possible. I prayed daily for guidance and strength.

The next day as I was retrieving our mail, and my neighbor, Jane, asked how I was doing. I burst into tears and told her I had just found out my husband has terminal cancer. She lovingly put her arms around me and told me she would support me in any way she could. This special woman became my *angel*. Jane was a constant source of comfort and strength for me. Her sense of humor was an immeasurable gift and brought much needed perspective.

This all took place the week of Christmas. Bobby sent the kids to get a tree, and he asked Sam to put the star on top. He was passing the tradition to his son. We had a lovely holiday meal, and Bobby toasted his last Christmas with us. We each put on a brave face which was made easier by Bobby's show of courage. He was handling his terminal diagnosis better than he had handled life!

We promised to make every day Christmas until the end. We enjoyed a poem he had written in a happier year:

Christmas Tree Friendship

Christmas trees are special trees
No two are alike
Their roots are multi-colored boxes
Meant to give delight

They're trees that need no water
Or sunshine to make them grow
They feed on decorated spheres and cones
And pastel lights that glow

Add a little tinsel
And an angel up above,
And as if by magic ... a Christmas tree is born
An ornamental structure ... built with love

Our being friends is much the same
It means so much to me
And if you stop and think awhile
We've built a Christmas tree!

Bobby

We continued golfing and socializing over the next few months. Once again, he told everyone he was dying. He gave some of his personal belongings away. I tried to be an observer as much as possible. I did not leave his side unless he was golfing with friends. Our relationship was serene and quite lovely during those months. I remember toward the end, there were a couple of very difficult emotional outbursts. I was quite willing to overlook them given the circumstances.

We celebrated being friends again. I admit that keeping my emotions in check was a challenge as I fought overwhelming sadness. A part of me was frustrated to know that he had the ability, all along, to be more stable and loving.

We both knew we had reached the end of our relationship as we knew it. He told me, "I would rather die than get a divorce. It will make better press." This type of theatrics was so typical of him. At a deep level, I knew it was true. He could not bear another marital failure, especially with me. Choosing more realistic expectations gave me serenity.

There were a couple of hospitalizations to treat the symptoms of the advancing cancer. Most of the time, fatigue was the major issue. With cancer, the blood thickens, and stroke risk is very real. He was put on blood thinners. We made two trips to the hospital for blood transfusions. He pushed himself to get out every day and play golf. As the end was near, he began to exhibit extreme weight loss. This is called cachexia and is a symptom of late stage cancer.

He called our daughter in San Diego and asked our son, who was still living at home, to both get on the phone with him. He said, "I am going to say goodbye to you now. I don't know how much time I have left, but it can't be much. I don't want either of you in therapy pounding pillows because I didn't say goodbye to you. I love you, and it's been a great ride." They each tearfully told him that they loved him as well.

He began to have difficulty digesting food. I knew his digestive tract was shutting down. He now spent most of the time in bed resting. I asked him if he would like to see photo albums of our life together. He said, "No, but I would like to look at the photos of my father and brother." I found it interesting that he wanted to see the faces of those he would be meeting up with on the other side.

I said, "You must be earning upgrades in Heaven after all this pain and suffering."

One day he looked at me and said, "I am not worried about you. Soon you will have another husband, a dog, and a motorhome."

I chuckled, "Oh Honey, that is the last thing on my mind. You'll have to *send* someone if that is going to happen. I don't think I will ever marry again." I found it a strange prediction since we didn't have a dog, and certainly this city boy and I had never camped or been in a motorhome. His idea of an adventure was running barefoot through a hotel. I vividly remember the last time we made love. His energy level was now so low that it was merely a gesture on his part.

I had learned some valuable lessons from the loss of my first mate regarding the final arrangements and funeral homes. I did not want to deal with the stress of making these decisions after his death. I got on the phone and began calling mortuaries. I found one which was owned and run by an old Italian family. I knew Bobby would like that. I took a drive to the facility and met the director. This was a lonely day for me. I told him we wanted cremation and how important it was to me that his body be handled with respect and care. I wanted it cremated on the third day, and I would be present. I signed all the papers, and I found it a great relief that these decisions had been made. I knew Bobby was not up to this discussion.

I called a hospice organization and asked questions. I wanted to be prepared if there was time to use them. They told me most clients waited too long to make this decision. They assured me there was much they could do to ease his final transition.

I had a lucid dream about James: *He leaned over and whispered in my ear, "Sherry, I will always be your best friend."* Remembering I had always said that I lost my best friend when he died, I knew he was at my side and would support me through the days ahead. I distinctly felt his presence and assistance when dealing with the hospital and physicians.

Two days before his last hospitalization, Bobby said, "I wish we hadn't fought so much. If only you had been different." Oh my gosh, I couldn't believe he said that! I went next door to my now good friend Jane and told her what he said. She burst into laughter, and we literally became hysterical at the great cosmic joke. I want to tell you he was kidding, but he didn't crack a smile. Perception is everything in life … was this how he saw our relationship? This is classic projection, seeing in another what you cannot face in yourself.

Toward the end of his days, I encouraged Bobby to compose more poetry for me. He said, "I will write to you from the other side." He did not disappoint.

One beautiful spring evening, Bobby asked me to go practice putting with him. Standing on the putting green, his breathing became very labored, and he had to sit down. As we drove home, I knew it would be our last time together in the golf cart. The desert sunset was spectacular that night. I put my head on his shoulder and silently wept as he drove his golf cart for the last time.

He was admitted to the hospital the next morning. On the way, he told me he was finished with treatment. "You've been through enough. It's time for me to die." I knew it was futile to say anything. He needed a reason to let go. It was a miracle he didn't die at home that night because his lung had collapsed.

The doctor put in a chest tube, and he immediately felt better. This was a traumatic yet necessary procedure. The resulting problem was that the tube couldn't come out. The doctor tried a painful procedure to try and seal the lungs, but it was not successful. The physician told me there was no more they could do. Bobby began to go into respiratory failure that night. The doctor wanted to put him on life support because he had not signed a Do Not Resuscitate form. I got extremely upset and pleaded with them to let him die in peace. I threatened to carry him out of the hospital if they would not honor my request. Fortunately, they were reluctantly willing to hear my plea.

I called the kids and told them it would not be long before their dad died. I quietly sat at his bedside that day as he waited for them to arrive. Meanwhile, I called in hospice because he said he wanted to go home. I slept on a mattress on the floor just as I had always done with his hospitalizations. I was so tired from the sleep deprivation and the stress. I felt like I was living in a hazy dream. Some of our friends came to see him, and I found their presence very comforting.

We took Bobby home on hospice care. I remember the ride home quite vividly. He was slumped over in the seat and barely able to breathe. I silently shed tears all the way home.

When we arrived, our son Sam was waiting to help me get him into the house. We managed to put him in the wheelchair and move him into the bedroom.

I had a team of people setting up the hospital bed in the living room. This would allow him to see his beloved golf course. I had no idea how long he would live. Sam sat with him and, after a few minutes, he called to me that his dad was turning blue. I had forgotten to turn the oxygen back on when we got him into the house. Bobby always joked that one day I would kill him!

When I returned to the bedroom, I witnessed the most touching and unforgettable scene.

When Sam was a child, Bobby always sang *It's Only a Paper Moon* (Harold Arlen) to him as a lullaby. Bobby's father had sung it to him. He thought it would be a special tradition to pass on.

Sam then held his dad's hand and sang the same lullaby to him. "*It wouldn't be make believe if you believed in me.*" Sam said, "I believe in you Dad. You are my super hero ... the strongest, bravest man I have ever known. You can go now, and I know you will be fine. You have taught me well. I love you so much, and I always will." Now that's something few nineteen-year old men would think to do at such an emotional time. Obviously, Sam is a very special guy with deep love for his dad.

We got Bobby into bed with the help of the hospice nurse. She showed me how to administer the morphine and breathing treatments. He was semi-comatose at this point and drifting in and out of consciousness. To our surprise, Bobby sat bolt right up in bed and said, "I want to get out of here!" He was quite distressed and confused. I managed to get him settled down and medicated again.

Alysia, Sam, and I spent a quiet evening with him, talking to him and telling funny stories from the past. I slept on the couch and monitored his condition. He was at peace. I softly reminded him over and over again, "I will always love you. You are not going to get better. You can go now. Follow the light ... Everything is fine ... I will always love you." Knowing that his insatiable need to be loved was a dramatic theme in his life, I wanted to remind him that he was truly loved by me.

He survived the night. In the morning, a hospice worker came and bathed him. He lost bowel and bladder control, and his skin began to have a mottled bluish appearance. I knew the end was near. Alysia was helping me turn him when he looked up at her then winked and smiled. That was his last loving gesture to his daughter.

I phoned all of his very best friends who lived quite far away. I told them he was actively dying. I asked that they start praying for him. Each of them had a message of love or a story to relay to him. He had a circle of heart centered friends, and they loved him unconditionally. I told him each story, knowing that the ability to hear is present until the end. I continued reminding him, "I'll always love you."

I wondered if this was all there would be for us. No final parting words? And then it happened. He managed to open his eyes. He looked intently at me and tried to speak. I could not make out what he was saying. There was no strength left to project the words. I put my ear up to his lips and asked him to please tell me again. He faintly whispered, "*You are so beautiful.*" Those were the last words he would ever say to me. They were quite enough. He finally recognized me as his lover and friend just as he had in the beginning of our time together.

A family of close friends came to see him one last time. I sent our kids out on an errand. As I let our friends out the door, they called back, "Goodbye Bobby, we love you." When I went back to his bed, he was gone. So easily had he slipped out. This man who made so much noise in life was so serene in death.

The hospice nurse was in the next room. She propped his chin up with a towel. We had dressed him in his favorite shirt with a rainbow on it. It all seemed so fitting. He had always signed his letters with "*Have a rainbow of a day.*" He came into our life on a rainbow and left the same way. It was May 5th.

When the kids came home, we all gathered around his body. We talked about him and to him, sensing he was still in the room. I said, "I love you so much. At times, you drove me crazy, yet I always loved you." There was great truth in my words.

Jane came over along with Rich. They said their parting farewells. The mortuary came to retrieve his body. He was so difficult for the attendants to lift. In my feeble attempt to lighten the somber mood I said,

"Hmmm, I wonder if this is what they mean by *dead weight?*" I smiled, and they just looked at me like I was insane.

Three days later, Jane and I went to the mortuary. I took a final look at his body before they slid it into the oven. I felt at peace. We went to lunch at a nearby restaurant, talked about his life and toasted him while his shell was burned to ashes. I later took them home in a box. This was what he had requested. I called it my box o' Bobby.

We opted for no memorial service since most of our loved ones lived out of the area. I wrote a story about his life and sent it to our friends all over the globe. A month later, we had a dinner in his honor at his favorite Italian restaurant. His closest family and friends were in attendance.

I was immersed in the laziness of grief and numb from all the trauma. I now felt free to share the entire truth of how difficult the last chapter had been. I did not miss the years of dysfunction and stress in my life, but I grieved the loss of his passionate presence. Experiencing tremendous relief at the closure of his suffering did bring peace. I continued to feel intense gratitude for the love and support in my life which once again lifted me up.

CHAPTER 19

Making Sense of It All

***Death is not only a time of mourning.
It is a time of truth.***

~Emmanuel's Book

I felt drawn to visit my most valuable support person during those challenging years. The psychologist who knew us so well warmly embraced me. I don't think I have ever cried so hard or intensely as I did that day in the therapist's office. It felt like the years of pent up anger, sadness, frustration, and confusion came pouring out of my soul in one swift rush of emotion. I felt completely safe in his presence. This was the wise, old soul, who came into my life to both guide and somehow give me protection from the raging storms my family often experienced. His office was like a sanctuary to me. I would always find a way to see him when I had exhausted all of my other resources. This was my salvation when dealing with this challenging and complicated life. He was my guardian angel in the flesh.

On this day, I blurted out the entire story. I had always gone to him for advice and guidance. Today was different. It was over, and another chapter of my life was behind me. With Bobby deceased, I could ask questions I never dared ask before. In the past, a part of me didn't want to know the answers. These answers would force me to look at our relationship truthfully and make decisions I hadn't been ready to live up to. I believed that disentangling from marriage to this man would be close to impossible. Loving him was the *higher path.*

"You never came to me for marriage counseling because you *knew* your marriage would *never* survive that kind of scrutiny." He was correct. If I ever told the *entire* truth of what went on behind closed doors, no therapist alive would advise me to stay in this marriage. I told him that my heart kept changing my mind, and yet I often longed for a less complicated life. The work of adult life is not easy!

I asked, "What was Bobby's diagnosis?" I knew he had a personality disorder. I knew it all too well.

"He had a borderline personality, and he was dissociative." There were also other qualities to his personality that defied logic or understanding. This intelligent, experienced, and understanding guide had heard many of our stories over the years.

I asked, "In the beginning, you were so positive of our chances of success. Why?" He said, "I believed in *you* Sherry and in the power of *love*. I often worried that I had been overly optimistic. Please forgive me."

What about my children? Will they ever be able to live emotionally healthy lives? I felt so guilty at times for having exposed them to such a complicated life.

I truly believed their life would be more difficult if I divorced. "Don't concern yourself over the welfare of the kids. There was always love and forgiveness in your family even in the face of such painful dysfunction. They will heal, and they will be just fine. This crisis is another turning point." His predictions had always come to pass, so I was feeling quite comforted.

I finally gathered myself together and was calm again. I blurted out the other question on my mind. "What do I do with my life now?" I've buried two husbands. I was only fifty yet felt much older that day. Plenty of men and women have more tragic stories than I do, yet I was definitely feeling a degree of battle fatigue.

"Write a book." That was what he said. "There are other people who have experienced, will experience or *are* experiencing these things. They need to hear your story. Remember, every ending is part of a beginning." I promised to seriously consider the advice. I definitely come from a family of story-tellers. I was always the teller of truths much to the chagrin of my parents.

I phoned UCSF and asked to speak to the physician who had handled Bobby's first cancer treatment. I updated him on Bobby's death and diagnosis. I asked why a more complete workup, to look for more cancer, had not been done. He thanked me for the follow-up information. He compassionately explained to me that when there is one cancer often more types of cancer exist in the same body. Their goal was to treat the most serious presenting symptoms. I felt closure understanding more completely the bigger picture.

I believe there is a period of time after crossing over to the next life that increased opportunities for communication exist. I have been careful not to expect such communication yet to stay open to the experience if it arises. By remaining detached and staying in the present moment, I believe I have been in a more receptive mental state.

Bobby knew, all too well, of my communication with James. Being the competitive mate that he was, I was quite curious to see if he would find a way to give me any final message from the here-after. We had discussed it over the years, and he knew I would welcome any sign from him. It had been a couple of weeks since his crossing. I was starting to miss him a great deal. I still had the box of his ashes in my closet. I wanted to find a resting place for them. Occasionally, Bobby would joke with me and the kids about his eventual death.

He would say, "There are twenty-four hours in a day, and I expect the three of you to each take eight-hour shifts crying over my grave." I decided that I should find a special burial place rather than scattering his ashes.

I took a trip from my home in La Quinta to Newport Beach to visit my brother and his family. While there, my sister phoned one night. She was quite excited and a little distraught. Raunell said she had received a communication from Bobby. I was thrilled and said, "Give me *every* detail."

She told me she had been working on her computer when the lamp next to her began to flicker off and on. Next, her computer screen went blank followed by a screen filled with random words. It was as if it were trying to reboot itself. Finally, only the word *phoenix* appeared at the top left of the screen. A distinct inner voice said, *"**Tell her to remember the phoenix.**"* And then the experience was over.

Just as the first message from James came to my mother, this first communication from Bobby came to my sister. She did have a special connection to Bobby. She is also very intuitive. The message made perfect sense to me. Over the years, I had both thought and said to Bobby, "Our relationship is like the mythical phoenix rising from the ashes." This love was stronger than our wounds and ego conflicts. The phoenix also represents the Christ. The cremation seemed to tie in with the idea of the phoenix. This was his confirmation of life after death. My sister knew nothing of the phoenix. Only Bobby and I shared that knowledge. A few days later, a white van pulled up next to her. The wording on the side was: *The Church of Phoenix, where you are loved and accepted*. This was another meaningful coincidence.

Following this conversation, I had the thought to ask my brother about a cemetery in Newport Beach. I hadn't been thinking along those lines before this. He said we were going to visit a friend the next day who lived above a lovely cemetery. We checked it out. There was a beautiful cremation garden, perched high on the hillside, overlooking the ocean. Bobby and I spent an incredible vacation in Newport Beach just the previous year. The spot overlooked this very coastline area. It was the perfect location for his remains. I immediately bought a plot and ordered a headstone which read, *Loving-Husband-Father-Friend.* This is exactly how he wanted to be remembered. To the very best of his ability, I truly believed he worked at this.

Later that week, I was feeling rather blue one day, and I decided to write Bobby a letter. I knew this form of journaling was a powerful way to process emotions. Upon finishing my letter to him, I felt a strong urge to write. It was as if he were there with me. The words flowed through my mind to my pen. After I finished the writing, I was able to read and comprehend what I had written.

I have no history or experience of automatic writing. Bobby definitely had the gift of expression. The next several days, his energy was all around me. I experienced communication with him through scribing the words he fed me. To this day, I marvel at the gift he was able to give from the next life.

During his illness, Bobby identified strongly with his Italian heritage. In lieu of an emotionally healthy family, he gleaned pleasure from his Italian heritage which he clung to during his life. We listened quite often to Italian music and the song Volare' would not leave my consciousness for the entire week:

Let's fly way up to the clouds
Away from the maddening crowds
We can sing in the glow
Of a star that I know of
Where lovers enjoy peace of mind.
Let's leave the confusion
And all this illusion behind
Just like birds of a feather
A rainbow together we'll find
No wonder my happy heart sings
Your love has given me wings.
Dominico Modugno

I sat with pen in hand and this is the beginning of the communications which flowed through my mind:

Sherry,

"Just start to write and the words will flow. I am with you always. Life here is amazing ... free of pain, worry, and guilt. The light is so bright, and the love is so pure. The God force is all around and knowledge is pure and available to all seekers. You have many more miles to walk on the earth. There is more joy for you.

Trust and be patient. Let your grief flow out of you like a river to the sea. Let it cleanse you of the past, for now is all you need for perfect peace. I am, more than fine, as Jan used to say! You loved me well and I am sorry I fought your love so much and put conditions on it. I didn't understand, but it is all clear to me now.

I am continuing to evolve here, and you were right about the upgrades. The pain of the disease helped me work off some lower choices I had made. Thank you for standing by me, even when you wanted to leave. Thank you for enduring the anger you felt and thank you for believing in me, most of all. You were the only one who ever did.

Be at peace little one. God in heaven is watching over you and the children. I will be with you always ... so is James. His love abides as does mine. Your two guardian angels will show you the way. Your time is far off in earth years and that is good. You deserve the life that is coming to you. Rejoice and celebrate life.

Our marriage was a success. Write your book ... just tell the truth ... it will set you free. The poems will come, and I will help you." ~ **Your Devoted Bobby**

I was shaken by the experience. It was as real as anything in my life had ever been. I knew his passionate energy. He was present in the room with me, just as large in spirit as he had been in this earth life!

The next morning, I again awoke to Volare' playing in my mind. I could clearly hear the melody in my inner ear. I felt he once again was wanting to communicate. It is summer solstice and a solar eclipse as well. I held the pen in my hand ready to scribe his words:

> *The rain of time drops softly on the day*
> *Eternity cannot be measured*
> *But our love can fill oceans*
> *It is endless ... it is timeless*
> *It is a fluid ... living ... breathing ... love*
> *And its breath is feeding the universe*
> *A life force sent from God.*   ~**Bobby**

This was the first poem from the other side just as promised. The following morning was the same experience:

Sherry,

"*God grants all wishes in due time. One life leads to another. One love overlaps with another. It is all the same. The lessons are simple in nature yet difficult to complete. God is patient. The universe is timeless. Life is a gift. Use it wisely. Don't judge. It only brings pain and stunts your growth. Trust God. His love is unconditional, and he created all life. There is confusion on the earth and pain and sorrow, but in the end, God's plan will be fulfilled, and all will find the light, for our great creator will see that all life is redeemed. Ask to be shown your plan. It is all that is in your power. Lead by example, just as together we loved and learned and walked the earth. God is pleased and so am I. I love you my friend."* ~**Bobby**

The next day I was vacuuming the house and a voice inside my mind begins talking: "*Your love was like one of your massages.*" It seemed so odd and the phrase just kept repeating until I sat down with pen in hand:

Your love was like one of your massages
Amazingly sensual
Often pleasurable
Irritatingly silly
Always deep
Mostly satisfying
Terribly therapeutic
Extremely revealing
Forever left me coming back for more! ~**Bobby**

It is June 24th ... our wedding anniversary. I awoke to this message:

Sherry,

"The climate of our love was measured by the emotional storms passing through when it should have been measured by the constancy of it. We were steadfast to the point of combustion! Indeed, our relationship was resurrected time and time again by the germinating seed of God's indestructible love. Once realized, it cannot be destroyed, only forgotten. Never forget the force that drove us ever onward in spite of our ego wounds and fear. That same force will bring us together again in God's way, and God's evolution is absolute perfection. Know this my love."
~ **Bobby**

On June 25th ... I awoke once again to the same Italian love song playing in my head. I asked myself, "Why the same song? Was it my own imagination?" Immediately, the song switched to a different Italian song as quickly as if the CD button had been pushed! I asked if there was a message and the answer was *yes*:

Sherry,

"I overplayed it ... the family thing. The children were my touchstone to the past. I wanted that childhood which was taken from me, so badly, I would stop at nothing to get it back. In my zealousness, I often pushed too hard. Tell them I am sorry for the times

my desire cut like a knife. I love them so. Tell them I believe in them, I always did. From this side, their lights shine so brightly. It is a magnificent thing to behold and I am honored to have shared their journey. Tell them to believe in themselves. I live inside them and will guide them to their destiny. Stand firm for them my love." ~ **Bobby**

This was followed by a salutation to the kids:

Sam and Alysia,

"You were a thing of beauty to me ... your innocence ... your infinite potential ... I wanted it for myself. I envied your journey ... the love that surrounded you. I wanted to be bathed in the beauty of your lives. Sometimes I was blinded by that desire. For those times ... forgive me my loves. For all the rest ... I did my best." ~ **Daddy**

I then remembered him tap dancing (with his hands) on the counter top at work with Alysia's first tap dancing shoes. She was four. This was followed by a memory of him carrying Sam in the door as a baby of about eight months. I also flashed a memory of him taking all of us to the park and letting the kids play on the equipment.

June 26th ... another early morning awakening to an Italian love song:

My Darling,

"The love I feel for you is expanding in such a way that my light is filling the void that was once my reality. I was there with the therapist and the truth was spoken. We have a powerful bond, you and me. Our laughter, our love, and our ability to withstand the challenges of our world are proof. Never doubt that my love. Be at peace. Turmoil and strife were the paths we chose to learn through. Things are not as they appear on the earth. All conditions are opportunities for advancement ... Love is always the lesson. Forgiveness, joy, generosity as love and dedication are but a few of the conditions the human can experience under the umbrella of love. God Is Love. He protects us from darkness. He is the light. We are all love." ~Bobby

This poem followed:

Bygones ... What a great word
It reminds us to let go
Just turn away from the past
The only lesson the past has to teach is through
forgiveness in the present
Giving is only possible by forgiving

It is yours for the taking

Yet you must want the peace it brings with all your heart

and every fiber of your being

You deserve this blessing

This state of grace

Your garden can only grow with the fertilizer of forgiveness

Then water it with the love that will spring forth from your heart

And watch the panorama of beauty unfold! ~**Bobby**

At this point, a little more background information is useful. Bobby was such a comedian. He would go to any lengths to entertain. Often, he was told that he could pursue comedy professionally. He would quickly decline saying he didn't have any desire to entertain on stage:

To all of you ... (Sherry, Alysia and Sam)

"Regarding friendship and laughter: the greatest quality I have is my ability to stimulate laughter and lightness in others. Combined with good intent and God's infinite wisdom, it is a true gift. I tried to use it wisely. The reason I did not want to stimulate laughter in crowds was because my humor was directly tied to the unconscious needs and desires of others. I could only sense that in small numbers. I have left all of

you with that gift. The laughter has not left your lives just because I have expanded to the next dimension. Laughing and loving are synonymous. God is present at these times and is well pleased when his children are joyous. Laugh well ... laugh often ... help others do the same. This is my gift to you."

~ Daddy

This was immediately followed by another poem:

Loved ones:
Laughter is like a sneeze
It clears the passages of debris collected by the trials of life
The harder you laugh ... the more Christ can flow through you
This pure light will cleanse and heal you
It shines through you ... lighting the path for others
Your part is to desire lightness and laughter in your life
It is easy to be burdened by all the hurdles in front of you
If only you could know that laughter is like the dynamite of the universe
It has the power to clear the way for easier passage on your journey
It comes from God

You are the closest to him when you are enjoying his creation

All that lies within it

Be joyous my loves

Soon enough you will be dead weight. ~*Bobby*

This confirmed he was in the room listening as the funeral home retrieved his body.

June 28th ... I can't sleep ... *Volare'* is playing in my head:

Sherry my Love,

"The frenzied pace at which my mind raced against time, was ever driving me toward my destiny ... to know love ... total complete acceptance. I longed for it. From the moment of birth, I began searching for my heavenly birthright. The life I chose was my trial. God placed me here to struggle against man's inhumanity to man. I became the very essence of discontent. It must have been exhaustive to live in the wake of my tumultuous journey. I only knew peace in the comfort of your embrace, late at night, protected by the blanket or your understanding, and the steadfastness of your love. Thank you, Sherry, for those tranquil moments. You were my salvation. Thank you, God, for giving me the gift of her love."
~**Bobby**

The next communication came Christmas day of the same year:

My Dearest Sherry,

"I am with you always. Our past life together is bathed with love, forgiveness, and understanding. It was a necessary journey for our souls. Much karma was cleared. All that remains is love. It is all there is. You can move on now. I love you. I always have and always will. We did set an example. May the peace of Christ fill your heart as you remember our last Christmas together. Your beauty is infinite."~ **Bobby**

My emotional body was still scarred, and the flashbacks of traumatic experiences would continue for several years. The peace and understanding of our journey together has never left me. There are decisions in my life that I would change if I could. The spiritual lessons of love that my life with Bobby provided were priceless.

One week later, my sister and I were on vacation in Carmel. We were walking down the street and she said, "What's *Volare*'? There's a song playing in my head, and I don't know it." I laughed and told her about it being a favorite Italian love song of Bobby's. He must be here with us. The song title means *to fly*.

I then felt a strong nudge to go into a book store a half block away. I walked right up to a shelf and saw a children's book called, ***I'll Always Love You*** by Hans Wilhelm. It's a book about death! It was just another Bobby encounter directed from the other side. There is so much synchronicity in life. It can be quite entertaining if you choose to open your eyes and ears to experience it.

Several years later, I had a visitation dream with Bobby: *He came to me sobbing and apologizing with deep remorse and humility. He asked my forgiveness. Alysia is present in the dream. I forgive and release him. When I do this, her life passes before us. All of her wounds are healed bringing her to present time. (My act of forgiveness heals her past.)* This was not a whisper, this was a shout from the other side!

Looking back at this period of my life, I realize that my *essence* gave me the opportunity to be molded emotionally and spiritually. I had created the perfect conditions to face my own shadow and experience spiritual growth. This was at a frenzied pace. I faced it with courage, at times doubt, and always had the belief that I was exactly where I was meant to be. I instinctively knew when the lesson was coming to an end. Miraculously, I underwent a tipping point in my evolution. I was never alone. *Higher Guidance* was at all times lighting my path.

As I sorted through the remnants of my life, I searched for deeper meaning and understanding. The answer was shining brightly in front of me. Our lessons of love and belief in family emanated from the hearts of our children. They were strong and stable beacons of light. I felt infinite gratitude, certain my karma with Bobby was complete. I now knew peace. I put this chapter of my life to bed and moved on.

PART THREE

CHAPTER 20

LOVING GUIDANCE

*Have enough courage to trust love one more time
and always one more time.*

~Maya Angelou

It was July. I was starting to embrace the solitude and adventure of being single again. I liked the freedom it afforded me. My emotions were beginning to stabilize even though I was in a melancholy state much of the time. It was a rebirthing time, and my heart was wide open to each new experience. I fully realized that I had the opportunity to reinvent myself and my life if I chose to. It still felt bizarre to be single and a widow … again.

I decided I would not even consider dating until I felt whole and healed. I remembered all too well the urgency I felt the first time I was widowed. It really didn't matter if I ever married again. I did have a fantasy that it would be nice to have one soul mate relationship which did not involve so many lessons! Nevertheless, my life was in *God's* hands. I gave thanks every day for the opportunity to begin again. I decided to focus on my wonderful, loving, friends and family.

I received this message in meditation:

***Without judgement, every encounter becomes
a delicious adventure into the unknown where all
gifts reveal themselves. There is a lightness of spirit
which accompanies oneself through what was once
feared and avoided. Gifts of the spirit come wrapped
in suspicious circumstances. Suspend judgement and
see the light as it illuminates your true path. Feel the
hand of your spirit guide lead you in the direction only
detachment can reveal. Peace, joy, and understanding
await you ... Love is always the lesson.***

Within the week, I found myself in a lucid dream:
*I met a man with distinctive blue eyes. Over the years, I
had dreamt about this blue-eyed man before. There was
always recognition and love between us. This time, the
feelings of attraction were quite strong. We sat across
a table from each other exchanging information about
ourselves when a woman entered the room. She was a
wise woman figure and I knew her well. I was in awe of
her spiritual beauty.* **When you looked into her eyes,
you could see all the way to heaven**. *I embraced her
and began to introduce her to this man. She smiled,
and they exchanged a knowing and loving look at each
other.*

*She said, "I see you have met my son." When she
said these words, I instantly knew everything I needed
to know about this man. If he was her son, then he was
everything I had hoped to find spiritually. Later in the
dream, she was telling me that he was fifty-six years*

old, and he had been in school. I took this to mean he had been doing some important life lessons.

The memory of the dream stayed with me over the next several months. I wondered if it was a specific guidance dream which held clues to meeting up with another love. I began to realize I was indeed being lead to my next life.

In the fall, my cousin Patrick's wife encouraged him to invite me on a retreat to Hawaii. I was starting to have more energy and decided it would be an adventure worth taking. Under the umbrella of Patrick's unconditional love, I began to restore myself. The tropical breezes brought the healing and balance that only nature can provide. I felt cleared of the negative residue of my last chapter. We told stories and laughed in that cleansing way I needed so badly.

In December, my kids encouraged me to put my profile on Match.com. They had heard it was a great way to meet men and thought it would be fun for me. I was very resistant to the idea at first. When I realized I could remain anonymous for as long as I chose to, it seemed worth a try. I admit, my curiosity was piqued. I met a nice man and dated him a couple of times. I asked him to tell me about his mother and he said, "My mom is a real bitch. She is hateful and was a horrible mother." After finding out other things about him, I decided this was not the guy for me.

I looked, one more time, at the internet dating site. I thought, "We do so much online, why not look for a date who might become a mate?" I was particularly interested in the way men described what they were looking for in a woman. One common denominator was that so many men wanted a woman with a sense of humor. I certainly fit that bill!

By now, it was the first week of January. It had been seven months of experiencing my aloneness. My computer alerted me, "You've got mail." My pulse quickened as I saw the correspondence from a new man. He hadn't put his photo on the site, so I had to get to know him by his emails alone. As providence would have it, he had written to another lady first and the email was accidently deleted. Immediately, my picture popped up and he decided to write to me instead.

The rest is history. We were both looking for someone to date over the winter but certainly not a serious relationship. Famous last words. After a few days of corresponding, we decided to meet for lunch. My friend Jane said, "I have a good feeling about this guy. Go have a taco with him. What could it hurt?" She was taken by the fact that it was obvious he had a great sense of humor.

We decided to meet at the local Taqueria for lunch. He arrived first and, as I approached the table, he stood up to shake my hand. He had such a genuine, winning smile and a great handshake. I hate a limp handshake, and first impressions can be lasting. Within a few moments, we were chatting and laughing. An obvious easiness soon existed between us. I told him, "There is something you may want to know about me. I have buried two husbands."

He said, "That doesn't bother me. I have lost a wife as well."

After our congenial lunch, we decided on another date. He impulsively gave me a kiss as we parted. I was surprised by this forward gesture, yet it felt like two old friends had met up after a long time apart. The kiss did not seem inappropriate. He later said it was unusual, but he just felt compelled to kiss me!

Our first date was lovely. We had a romantic dinner under the desert sky. We chatted extensively about ourselves. We got all the history out of the way. We went to a club in Palm Springs and listened to a guitarist play the Blues. I discovered he was the sales manager for a company that converts buses to high end recreational vehicles.

He was also a musician/singer, having entertained professionally for much of his younger life. Leon had a hit record when he was fifteen. His life and history were quite interesting. He was; intelligent, sweet, sincere, fun-loving, funny, talented, and charismatic. There was definite chemistry between us. It was the warm, familiar kind. We knew immediately that we would be good friends. Early on, we both realized we were falling in love. No red flags this time, just a definite sense of belonging.

That night, I asked him to tell me about his mother. "My mother is sitting at the right hand of *God*. She was a very spiritually beautiful woman." I had goose flesh and chills running up and down my spine. He wanted to know why I asked. I took a chance on him understanding, and I relayed the dream to him. As I was telling him my dream, he began to actually shudder. The hair was standing straight up on his arms. He too had chills up and down his spine. We both knew in that instant that our meeting was *Divinely* guided. He was fifty-seven at the time. I later realized that he was fifty-six when I had the dream. I was certain that the wise woman in my dream was his mother guiding us.

We agreed to date exclusively until we had a chance to see where our relationship would go. After his first wife's death, he had experienced a difficult rebound marriage which ended in divorce. We were both feeling quite cautious where romantic relationships were concerned. Soon, it became obvious we were mutually ready to try again. One day, I was looking at him sitting on the couch. I realized being with him evoked a feeling of sweet comfort like coming home to myself.

There was never a reason not to be together. Since that first email correspondence, it's been an easy and fun life. It is one that is full of respect and adventure, much laughter, and most of all love. We share the same spiritual beliefs and commitment to family.

Our families blended together beautifully. Both of my kids loved him from the start. Our days always begin and end with a *thank you to God*. We both know we have been blessed in a very special way.

Leon and my son Sam share a love of music. Alysia loves him in a special way that only daughters can express. She told me after their first meeting that she would like to keep him for a friend if we didn't work out. My parents immediately bonded with my new love. What a delight to have so much harmony in my life. Most importantly, I love who I am when we were are together. I experience my authenticity without reservation. I soon discovered my capacity for love, intimacy, and joy had only grown over the years.

One lovely June day, we were cruising down the road in a bus with our beloved Duffy dog on my lap. I remembered those prophetic words Bobby spoke. "It won't be long before you have a new husband, a motor home, and a dog." His prophesy had become my reality. We married in November of that year, eleven months after our first date. We promised each other to always keep the good will alive in our relationship.

We are fond of saying, "We saved the best for last."

The first trip I made to Leon's home in Oregon was quite meaningful. We stopped in Reno and met his son, Jason, and family. We bonded quickly. Jason was happy to have one more mom to love. I felt a connection with the entire family. On our wedding day, Jason asked me, "Can I call you Mom?"

While at Leon's house, I was sorting out the kitchen and musing over his first wife's special dishes. There was a small painting on the wall that Jason had painted for his mom when he was a child. I spent some time thinking about her. I suddenly felt her presence in the room. She clearly had a message for me. ***"Thank you for loving my son. I will love him through you."*** The words were strongly imprinted in my mind. It seemed like quite an affirmation, and I knew that I recognized her spirit. I also realized how the strong love I immediately felt for Jason was influenced by her motherly love streaming through my heart.

Several years into our marriage, we discovered through DNA that Leon had an older son, Eric, and two grandchildren from a former relationship. This brought another dimension to the meaning of family. More people to love and embrace. We deeply appreciate our entire family.

Our life is interesting and always full of new experiences, friendships, music and laughter. Having a partner who shares similar perspectives of life is such a joy. Most importantly, supporting each other's spiritual growth has created respect and trust. I am truly blessed to have yet another opportunity to experience love.

Leon and I have been together for sixteen years at this writing. He has been a tremendous support to me during every crises and loss. There have been many during our time together. We often have open discussions about the eventual death of one of us. When that time comes, we know fully that we will be crossing from a legacy of love. Gratefully, our story is still being written.

CHAPTER 21

Amazing Mom

***The death of a mother is the first sorrow wept
without her.***

~Unknown

My mother was wonderful. There has never been
a more dedicated parent. She raised four children, one
with a serious disability. By the time I was twelve, she
had turned much of the household chores over to me.
This was in order to better care for herself and the other
children. Janet was; fun-loving, sensitive yet strong,
stoic, energetic and hard working. She was totally
dedicated to her husband and family.

Mom was amazingly psychic. She often talked
of her premonitions and dreams. Janet loved family
gatherings, and she also enjoyed playing a slot machine
now and again. My mom prided herself on self-control
and her appearance. She was quite social, loved to
shop, and was incredibly thoughtful.

This special woman was attractive and very well
preserved for her age. All of my dates in high school
commented on her beauty. She loved these compliments.
My mother gave birth to me at age eighteen. She was
my best friend for many years of my life. Mom could
be loyal to a fault, and she was always quite protective

of her children. All who knew her would tell you that she loved life and made the most of her years. This was in spite of much heartbreak along the way.

She insisted on having a strong and positive attitude and to always be very generous and helpful. Her best quality was that she loved to laugh. My fondest memories are of my dad making her laugh until she would pee her pants! She was long-suffering and lived with a serious neck injury most of her adult life. Her childhood was difficult due to the fact that her father died when she really needed him. My grandmother was mentally unstable and could be unkind.

My mom and my sister Janie discovered they had cancer with two months of each other. They always had what would be called an enmeshed and symbiotic relationship. This seemed somehow karmic. At her own request, Mom had a mastectomy and was treated extensively with chemotherapy. She would do anything to stay alive to support and look after my sister.

Mom's cancer went into remission, but her brain began to show signs of distress. This was believed to be from the trauma and side effects of the chemotherapy. The neurologist said she had *chemo* brain. This condition, coupled with the emotional stress of knowing my sister was gravely ill, was just too much for her. It seemed her brain went on tilt.

She relinquished Janie's care to my youngest sister who lived in the same town. Raunell agreed to now look after Janie's medical and other continual needs. Dad said he would care for Mom. This seemed reasonable at the time. As the years progressed, the demands on my younger sister from both Mom and Janie were extensive. She was a real trooper, willing to make any personal sacrifice to support them. I felt frustrated much of the time because I lived hundreds of miles away. I could only support them all by phone. I reassured my sister that I would come whenever she needed me.

It became clear, after a couple of years, that Mom's brain was getting progressively worse. She gradually lost her ability to negotiate the physical world and also lost her ability to perceive sight or direction. There was serious short-term memory loss. CT scans and an MRI lead to a diagnosis of Degenerative White Matter Disease along with Chronic Ischemic Disease. My dad made the decision not to share the diagnosis with my mom. It seems there is still so much shame associated with mental decline. Her disease was somewhat like Alzheimer's. All hormones were discontinued due to the breast cancer. We always wondered how lack of estrogen may have contributed to the degeneration of her brain.

She grieved the loss of her life as she knew it. She had always been a very social person and so full of life. Janet was a real estate agent and loved her job serving others. Due to her brain changes, she became more reclusive over the next few years, however, she never lost her desire to go to the beauty shop weekly. Her life, as she knew it, disappeared inch by inch. There was never a complaint but always a smile on her face.

Dad was, for the most part, amazing. As her vision vanished, she became totally dependent on him for every need. As her life became smaller and smaller, so did his. He eagerly accepted any relief from intimate family but rarely involved anyone else in her care. We pleaded with him to enlist more help. He stubbornly insisted he could care for her by himself. One can only imagine how weary he became with his daily responsibilities. Her dementia took away any ability to have the relationship they had once known. She was able to reason and remember the past. She *always* maintained her sense of humor. Thanks to their shared love of laughter, they often found humor in their daily predicaments.

Fortunately, I was able to spend several weeks with Mom over these declining years. We had always been such good friends. It was heartbreaking to lose the closeness and watch her become more childlike. I found it interesting that her spirit was always shining through. Our time was intimate and special. We helped her do a review of her life during this period. We told stories of our childhood and helped her recall memories. We affirmed our love and appreciation of her as a woman and as a mother. As her sight went away, we did our best to be her eyes. I found it so sad when I realized she would never again look at those special photos, saved over the years, or even gaze into the eyes of her husband.

As a result of her diminished vision, she spent more and more time quietly withdrawn and contemplative. Toward the end of her life, she seemed more and more at peace. I asked her once if she was having any interesting spiritual experiences. She said, "*Yes,*" and went on to tell me that repeatedly she was being told by *God* to **witness** for him. She asked me what I thought that meant? I suggested that perhaps it meant she wasn't supposed to hide away in embarrassment over her condition but to let her light shine! I went on to say she could allow the world to see how she was handling her illness with courage, grace, and dignity. These were spiritual qualities, true gifts from *God*. She could continue to do his work by using this illness to *witness*. From that time on, she stopped being embarrassed or unwilling to go out in public.

Mom was very frightened and confused at night. Trying to find her way to the bathroom was quite an ordeal. One night, when I was staying with her, I had this experience: As we lay next to each other in bed, I felt an energy fill the room. A voice spoke through me to her.

The guide said, **"*Janet, think of Jesus holding one hand and your guardian angel holding the other. Do this when you feel alone.*"**

She totally identified with her guardian angel and had a picture of an angel guarding a little girl and boy hanging by her bed. She loved the message and began using this imagery as her mantra. She chanted it often and said it brought her peace. She began to feel less afraid and lost at night.

About a year preceding her death, both Raunell and I began to have dreams about her dying. One was especially profound for me:

*My dad bought an executive home for them and he took Raunell, Janie, Mom and I to see it. We were riding in the back seat of a VW bug. We came to a Dead-End sign and he turned down a different road that took us straight up a mountain. At the top was an executive neighborhood, and we turned down the street named Del Monte (which means from nature or God). The house was lovely. He had furnished it with all their favorite, treasured belongings, even pictures of the family were hanging on the wall. There were books in the bookshelves. He told me to take my mom down the hall and show her their room. I lead her down the hall, then showed her the last room on the left. There was a **veil** hanging over the entrance. She was hesitant to go through the veil, so I held it aside and she went in. The room was beautiful, with a four-poster queen size oak bed and lovely furnishings complete with exquisite linens on the bed and curtains etc. There was an adult sized crib next to the bed with toys in it. She started fondling the toys. I said, "Look! He has made a bed for your baby." I knew it was a bed for my sister, Janie.*

I told my mom about the dream. She asked me what I thought it meant. I told her I imagined it meant she would die before Janie. She was going to a lovely place. She seemed to accept this interpretation without question.

My sister and I felt we were being given a gift in receiving these dreams. We had time to say goodbye. We prepared ourselves for an early passing of our mom. We each handled this in our own way. Even though my mom was not told outright of the seriousness of her condition, she slowly began to let go of this life.

She was concerned over the fact that she did not attend church any more. For her seventy-fifth birthday, we went to the Bible bookstore and bought several compact discs of her favorite old time spiritual hymns. We also bought her some symbolic stones to hold. Rubbing these pieces helped calm the nervous ticks she had developed. Dad would play the music for her every Sunday morning. This became her *church* experience. She was quite happy and comforted singing and humming those old familiar songs. It proved helpful to get creative to meet her special need.

Janet dearly loved her siblings and especially her younger brother. They had survived a difficult childhood together. Around this time, he died unexpectedly from a ruptured brain tumor. I will never forget taking her to the hospital to say goodbye to him. It was heart wrenching. I took some comfort realizing she would soon be joining him.

I believe that beginnings and endings are so important in life. As Raunell and I sensed the end coming, we became increasingly aware of Mom's condition rapidly progressing. She was losing her grip on this life, and her physical abilities declined dramatically. Her eyesight was now almost gone. Because she was only able to see shapes out of the corner of her right eye, she was very unstable on her feet. She couldn't remember how to get in the car. My sister was taking her to the beauty shop every Thursday, and she told me she didn't think it would be long before that would no longer be possible. This was quite distressing for Mom … her last outing taken from her. She was now falling regularly.

She repeatedly told us that she *refused to be an invalid*. I wondered what that meant to her. From my perspective, she was already an invalid. It turned out that the day she could no longer use her legs was the day she unarguably became an invalid. She cried on the way to the hospital, telling her youngest daughter that she was trying *so hard*. Dad had gotten frustrated the day before. He had brought home a different car for her to negotiate to no avail. She turned the last corner of her life. We had no idea the end was so close. Neither did the physicians. It was as if she willed herself out of this life. My strong-willed mother made her own rules for her exit time.

When I arrived at the hospital, she couldn't wait to tell me something. She said, "I've decided I have two choices. I can have a nervous breakdown, or I can be positive. I choose to be positive." My mom always used this as her strength throughout her life. She believed she could choose positivity in all circumstances. I knew how scared and heartbroken she was about the state of her health. This was her way of being brave. After another MRI and a complete work up, we were told her condition was in an advanced state and irreversible. The doctors didn't feel she would ever go home again.

Dad was not prepared for this news nor was he willing to accept it. He said, "They don't know our family."

The neurologist believed that we should consider comfort care only. He said it was because she was suffering now and would suffer more in the future. He advised, "Just let nature take its course." Doctors said she could live in this progressively worsening state for years. What a horrible thought. I knew I would do whatever I could to help her get ready to leave this life. I immediately began to think about hospice. The doctors agreed to consider hospice after she went to the nursing home for rehab. The rehabilitation stay was merely a formality to make certain that the use of her legs could not be restored.

I went to my parent's home to prepare the physical space for a hospital bed. We furnished the room in preparation of bringing her home on hospice care. Our dad was devastated. He turned these decisions over to my sister and me. He didn't have the heart or the courage to explain this to my mom. He was grieving uncontrollably.

The nursing home experience was a nightmare for her. She continued to be quite positive but had begun to show signs of serious withdrawal. We brought her a CD player and all her favorite music. This was the only activity that brought her comfort. She kept her eyes closed most of the time now. She only spoke when she was asked a question, and she was beginning to have more confusion. Our brother came. He said he felt that this was his goodbye. She told him she knew her son wouldn't let her down. He cried when he told me about their conversation. There was a sweet woman who shared Mom's room. She assured us each night that she would look after her. She followed through with the promise, and she often summoned the nurses if she thought Mom needed attention.

Mom developed a bowel obstruction in no time. While in the hospital, her pain levels had increased significantly requiring the use of narcotics. This in turn affected bowel evacuation. She began to throw up and required enemas and laxatives etc. The staff moved her in and out of the bed with a lift or by physically pushing and pulling her. They doused her daily in the shower and even yelled at her to evacuate. She was totally unable to follow these commands. I was aghast at their cold treatment of her.

One day she told my dad, "Get me out of here. I don't owe these people *anything* and I don't *deserve* this." My sister and I met with the neurologist to further discuss her brain scans. The white matter was extensively damaged. We were amazed that she was functioning at all. It quickly became obvious that she was not going to regain the use of her legs.

I asked my mom if she wanted me to explain to her about her condition. She said that she did. I imparted to her in the kindest most gentle way possible that her brain was continuing to get worse. We now needed a team of caregivers to look after her. I told her we were taking her home with the help of hospice. I asked if she understood and she said, "Yes my brain hasn't been right for a long time." This was a hard conversation for me, but she handled it with her usual dignity and courage. The doctor ordered hospice care, and she was discharged in a few days.

Leon and I returned home to Oregon. Raunell took total charge of the situation. She did a spectacular job getting her signed into hospice and all of the care lined up. This involved interviewing caregivers, setting up schedules, and taking care of Mom physically. It was a colossal effort working out the details since her care was quite extensive. Trying to get Dad to understand the changes that had taken place was a challenge as well. I spoke with him daily on the phone. It helped me feel a part of this phase. I fought the guilt over not being there, yet somehow knew this intimate time was important for my sisters. Our Aunt Jeanie started coming over daily to lend her support as well.

I wrote a letter to my Dad insisting he accept the nature of the situation. He was still in denial about the fact that she was nearing the end. I was afraid my sister would burn out. We needed him to snap out of his emotional distress and pitch in more. He was very reluctant to hire extra caregivers. Hospice only makes a handful of visits to guide and supervise medications and patient progress. He was hurt by my words for which I later apologized. It did seem to help ease the situation.

My sister began to share with me, daily, the changes and progression Mom was exhibiting. All indicators were that she was preparing to die and getting closer every day. She continued to keep her eyes closed, yet when she first arrived home and looked around the room she could see quite well. (This was interesting since she was almost totally unable to physically see.) She said, "We get to walk here for a while and then we go home."

A friend brought food over and as she left Mom said, "I have to remember what to say to each person." One day Raunell brought her puppy, Bella, over and she slept on Mom's abdomen. Mom said, "Bella is our angel. She is here to help us. It's too bad I won't be here to see her grow up." Mom talked about how important it is to care for our animals. She also told her to let her father in the door.

My sister queried, "Your father?"

She said, "*Yes*, my father. He's at the door. Let him in." He had been deceased since she was twelve.

When my sister told me these stories, I knew I needed to return right away. It was obvious, Mom was preparing to transition. Hospice said if there are daily changes then a person probably has days to live, if weekly then weeks. I drove back down. Before I left, I spoke with my brother and the grandkids. I told all of them that if they had anything they wanted to say to their grandmother to write to me, and I would read it to her. They did write, and when I read the letters to her she cried.

Before I arrived, Mom woke up one night, and she and my dad had a long intimate conversation. They hugged and kissed and discussed their love and life together. It was amazing that she became this coherent. This would be the last intimate conversation for them. My dad was on such a high after this happened because their previous conversations had been so scant. She then began to withdraw further.

When I arrived on the last day of October, she opened her eyes when I came in the room. I went over to her and she started pointing to her watch and she said, "*Truth, truth.*" I knew she meant that I had told her the truth, and there wasn't much time left.

I calmly said, "It's okay Mom, I understand. I will stay with you." I knew her time was close. I promised to take care of her until she was delivered into the next life. Being the nurse in the family, I always stepped in for these grave situations. I do not have special training for the care of a dying patient, but I have good instincts for what is needed. I was beyond grateful for the guidance of hospice nurses. It was dreadful to watch the suffering and decline from brain disease.

My mom told me she only had one regret about her life. She said, "I wish I hadn't been so vain." I assume she was referring to the pride she took in her physical appearance.

I'll add another aspect to this final chapter for my mom. My sister Janie came daily and observed all that was happening with Mom. I wondered what she was thinking as I watched her own life force waning. I knew my mom was crossing first in order to show Janie the way. It was as if she was willing herself out of this life. Janie was so strong. Her steadfast loyalty and love for my mom was quite touching.

Raunell had an experience. She could see slits of light all around her like the veil between worlds was getting thinner, and bright light was shining through. Each day, Mom's desire for food and then water diminished.

I would let the medication wear off and Dad would go in and talk with her during these more alert times. Even though she rarely talked, she would tell me when she wanted more pain medication. We gave her morphine liquid and crushed the other medications in applesauce. Eventually, we stopped all oral medication except for pain and discontinued offering food and water. This was a very difficult time. Dad wanted to keep trying to feed her. I sat him down and reminded him that we were not trying to get her to regain interest in this life. She was telling us she was ready to let go. We needed to have the courage to allow her. There was nothing but more suffering if she lived. It just felt so unnatural to stop trying and to give up hope. We were at the final stage of her illness and it was time to help her in a different way. I understood his confusion. I had to keep re-reading the hospice material myself. My sister and I were in constant attendance at her bedside.

I gave her a manicure and pedicure. We washed her hair. It took great tenderness to accomplish this due to her severe pain. She grimaced and groaned with each little move. I understood that this was part of the dying process. Thank *God* for narcotics when there is this level of suffering. One night she became very alert and she said, "Everyone seems really happy."

I said, "Yes they are. Mom are you happy?"

She said, "Oh *yes*, I am *so very happy.*" As she approached her *Heavenly* homecoming, she had her usual positive attitude.

The next day, she was totally unresponsive. Dad brought in the last two roses from the garden and put them in a vase by her bedside. He told her what he was doing. She would never talk to us again. We kept talking to her, realizing that she could still hear us. Her suffering increased, making turning her more traumatic. It broke our hearts to cause her any more pain, but it was necessary to avoid skin breakdown. We kept giving the morphine round the clock which did offer some relief.

The hospice nurses came and went, reassuring us each time. They were tremendously helpful in explaining the stages of dying. We were able to get her bowels evacuated and control much of the pain. Her state of consciousness decreased, but it was clear she could still hear. For days, her breathing pattern was erratic and one night we felt that she certainly would expire. Raunell spent the night at her bedside along with me. Her breathing was very noisy, a kind of grunting sound. It was so painful to listen to this death moan. It sounded like she was fighting to stay with us with each labored breath. Her chest was filling up with fluid. Obstetrics being my field, I noted that the process was much like a woman in labor. I kept coaching her, helping to birth her into the next life.

We turned her onto a more dramatic side position, and this seemed to ease her. At this point, when we turned her she opened her eyes fully and was moving them from side to side as if she saw something. She then half closed them for a few minutes. A moment before this, I saw a tear roll down her cheek. I felt she was understanding that she was leaving us. I wanted to cry but knew I had to be brave for her. I did my best to convey an atmosphere of calm confidence.

The next time we turned her, she looked quite lifeless to me. She had blue, mottled skin and was totally unresponsive except for the erratic breathing. It seemed her spirit had left her body, yet her body was still struggling. We kept talking to her and encouraging her. We said everything we could think of to give her permission to let go. We put headphones on and played her favorite Hawaiian music. It was my daughter's birthday, and I realized she would fight to live one more day. We cried, prayed, and were there for each other that long night.

She continued the distressful breathing for another thirty-six hours. It was the longest hours of our lives. My sister went home to freshen up. As she was leaving her house to return, she had a premonition to check on Tada, her Pitbull terrier. She found her beloved old dog suffering and knew she had to call the vet to euthanize her. Mom loved that dog. It was fitting they would transition at the same time. What an excruciatingly painful, traumatic day for my sister.

Dad had now accepted the finality of the situation. He sat at Mom's bedside and told her how he loved her and then urged her to let go. I told her she wouldn't get better now and to look around for the light. My brother and husband came. Janie was there every day. Other close family members came to say their final goodbyes. Everyone encouraged her to let go. She identified so strongly with her guardian angel. We visualized a funnel of light going from her bedside candle to the angelic kingdom and encouraged her to hop into it. This was cousin Patrick's suggestion. She was quite the stubborn woman in life. It was fitting that she would at some level continue to hold on.

Raunell was exhausted, therefore I encouraged her to go home and get some sleep. Before I went to sleep I told Mom, "Tada went to Heaven today and Raunell wants you to go take care of her." I kissed her and told her it was her time to go, and that she could come to us in our dreams any time she wanted. An hour later, there was silence in the room. I checked her and she was still quite warm, but she was gone. At the end, she was totally peaceful.

I woke Dad up and gave him the news. He jumped up and went to her bedside. He cried and caressed her. I called both sisters and my husband. Dad said, "I have to be strong for your sisters." I knew he needed to hold on to a sense of purpose in order to get through his devastation. I called everyone close to Mom.

Dad then did the most touching thing. He got a warm washcloth and washed her face. He gave me her favorite lipstick and I put it on her. We brushed her hair and arranged her in the bed. My sister was crying. Dad gave her the washcloth and told her to wash her tears with Mom's tears. Then he brought out one of Mom's favorite silk red outfits to clothe her body in the casket. I held back tears the best I could. I didn't want to miss a moment of this sacred experience.

I phoned hospice and fortunately my favorite nurse was on call. She came to the house, filled out the paper work and called the mortuary. Dad didn't want her body embalmed. We disposed of the leftover narcotics. The nurse insisted on doing this right away which is normal hospice protocol. The nurse managed to get Mom's rings off. The mortuary came about an hour later. They put her body in a red velvet bag. I was relieved they didn't cover her face as they took her body away. They were very respectful and appropriate. We gave them her clothing and instructions regarding how to fix her hair. We sent the last red rose Dad had picked to put in the casket as well as a stuffed dog to symbolize Tada. We told them the casket would be closed for the funeral.

I am certain I have forgotten much of what happened those last eight days. Many friends and neighbors stopped by with food and encouragement. We went to the funeral home and helped Dad pick out a casket. He asked if Leon would play music and sing at her funeral. He wanted me to give the eulogy. I knew I would certainly honor his wishes, yet I was so overwhelmed at this point. This was not going to be easy. I decided to tackle one task at a time. This is how I would get through it. Together we managed to put a lovely service together. Our Aunt Jeanie handled the gathering after the service. My brother's wife made a beautiful collage from family photos and an enlarged picture of Mom for by her casket. We put quotes from the grandkids in the pamphlet we handed out. It all came together quite nicely. I was tremendously grateful for all the help.

Friends from far and wide came. This was immensely comforting for my Dad. The hardest part of the situation for me was watching my Dad's pain. I felt honored to be at his side during their earth ending. They were married in their teens. I could feel Mom's presence. The intimate family had the casket opened before the funeral. Her body looked lovely even in death. Leon tenderly put one of his guitar picks in the casket. I smiled inwardly, knowing she was pleased. Several people said they sensed her presence during the funeral. My intuitive cousin said she was praying for each person as they walked by her casket. He also said he could see a projection of my Dad standing in front of the casket protecting her. Leon sang and played guitar. I don't know how he pulled it together to sing *One More Day*. It was lovely:

> *Last night I had a crazy dream*
> *A wish was granted just for me*
> *I could wish for anything*
> *I didn't ask for money*
> *Or a mansion in Malibu*
> *I simply wished for one more day with you.*

> *One more day, one more time*
> *One more sunset, maybe I'd be satisfied*
> *But then again, I know what it would do*
> *Leave me wishing still for one more day with you.*
>   Diamond Rio

I delivered the eulogy. I kept telling myself I was making her happy to create a service so fitting to her exemplary life. The most touching thing that happened to me that day was when my two kids came from the side family room to sit with me and hold my hands for support. We all have a special love for my mom. The grandkids were all so loving and sweet. It was a very touching experience to see the evidence of my mother's legacy of love.

After the service, we opened the casket one last time for the immediate family. The kids let seventy-five balloons fly and said their last goodbyes. They quickly disappeared into the sunlight. Later my Dad told me, "I was her protector." I took him out to the cemetery later that day. The flowers were on the grave. It was the final step. The physical part of this earth life for Mom was over. I knew she would want us to be positive, loving, and giving in remembrance of her. I prayed for strength during the entire ordeal, and I was able to stay composed and clear thinking. I thanked *God* for this ability.

A couple of nights after her passing, Mom and I had an encounter. I woke up about three and was thinking about the guardian angel picture hanging in my parent's bedroom. I was wondering about Mom and her deceased brother Richard. Immediately, a clear message came to me. It was spoken in my inner ear as if I had asked a question and she was there to answer. I could see a vision of what she was describing:

"My brother and I frolic in the fields (I saw rolling fields of flowers and had a sense of glee and playfulness.) My sisters and I sip tea in the morning sun. (I saw a scene of women lounging on a veranda. They were clearly just being lazy and enjoying each other's company).

Actually, I am more like a firefly crossed with a butterfly! (I had a sense of light and floating.) It is magnificent here. All the loved ones gather to watch, wait, pray for all of you. (I saw a scene of many beings gathered around a long table.) Trust life, the great schoolroom. Let love lead the way. These ideas come from the 'One'. We share great love dear daughter."
~**Mom**

The second visitation was the next night. I felt I was channeling a letter from Mom to Dad. I woke up with my body filled with energy similar to an out of body sensation I repeatedly experienced as a child. The words kept repeating, *My Darling Bob, My Darling Bob*. Leon said my skin was really *hot,* but I actually felt cold. I started writing and this is what came through me:

My Darling Bob,

"Sherry hears me just as I once heard James for her. Honey don't look for me in the old familiar places. This will only bring you pain and loneliness. I am with you now and will remain until your walk is complete. We are joined through our hearts and mine is very much alive. It is through our indwelling Christ selves that our love will always be a living breathing force.

Please do one thing for me. Let our own light shine and know that my light now shines through you. I now walk by your side and am tucked inside your heart. Only you will know I am there but all those you encounter will see our brilliance for we ascended above our egos to know God's love. This was the purpose of the illness.

Listen for me in the stillness of the early morning. It is me, my Darling, my Honey, who whispers reassurance in your ear. All is well.

Enjoy and appreciate the love and joy that surrounds you. Be positive for me. I will help you. God's plan is good and soon you will understand and have peace. Know that I am holding your hand now. You served me well. I love you Honey." ~**Janet**

PS "Your gift of humor sustained me during my darkest days. Use it to feed our dear loved ones who still walk with you. Live ... Love ... Laugh. Do it for both of us."

I then had a vision of her in the nursing home and she said:

"I was shown what my future would be if I chose to keep holding on and fighting. I realized that there was no karma with these people. There was nothing to be gained by further suffering. I owed these people nothing. I realized that my peace would come by having the courage to let go and trust God completely. I am now whole."

She went on to say, "I am here with Emma (Leon's mother). We know her! She is delighted at your union."

When I told Leon, he became emotional and said, "That is exactly what my mom would say."

I gave the written correspondence to my dad. He kept it close and read it many times over the following years.

I continually sense my mom whispering in my ear. She is often laughing. I miss her physical presence, yet I know she is guiding and guarding constantly. For this I am grateful. A loving mother is forever a thing of true beauty.

CHAPTER 22

An Observer's Challenges

A sister is a gift to the heart, a friend to the spirit, a golden thread to the meaning of life.

~Isadora James

My sister Janie, was a solid supporting figure in our family. She was a dear sweet soul full of life, intelligence, and promise. When she was four, she began having grand mal seizures and was hospitalized at Stanford University. There was never any effective control of the condition. She was forced to live her life heavily drugged. The entire family was affected. Our parents were truly devastated and heartbroken.

Janie and I shared the same bed during that time. I vividly remember cradling her in my arms at night, as she seized violently, always losing bladder control. We would both be soaked in urine by morning. I felt true compassion for her.

Janie was so much more than her disability. She had a keen interest in photography and architecture, loved music, dancing, and was quite a craft person. She was extremely curious about life. Getting to know her true *essence* was a challenge because she was very shy. This shyness, coupled with all the drugs, caused her to communicate on quite a delay. With time and patience, intimacy could be achieved. She was strong, stoic, loving, and often very stubborn. Hers was a life of observing others most of the time. I believe she learned by watching and listening.

She eventually would fall in love and was totally dedicated to her man. Her partner called her the *general*. She would need every ounce of that strength to cope with her medical issues. My parents lived close by in order to support her varied needs. Every day was a struggle for Janie, yet I never heard her complain. She loved her life.

Following what seemed to be an upper respiratory infection, she developed a deep chest cough. Her symptoms were diagnosed as left lower lobe lung cancer. Back to Stanford she went. This was not a smoking related cancer. She had surgery to remove the affected lobe. This was an agonizing experience. Doctors gave her hope for a full recovery. Unfortunately, before the year was out it was discovered on PET scan that the cancer had spread to other parts of the lung. Without treatment, the prognosis was four years to live. She chose to forego any chemotherapy. She was already on so many drugs for the seizures, and she stubbornly did not want to endure any more side effects. Janie survived seven more years.

I clearly remember taking her to see a radiologist oncologist. He showed us the picture of her lung scan to review. The doctor very calmly showed her that there was no treatment available because both lungs were infiltrated with cancer. My heart sank. She handled it with her usual quiet dignity. On the way home I said, "Janie you will live as long as you want to. It is critical not to ever give up hope."

She said, "I am not afraid to die. I've already done it." She went on to tell me of an experience when she was in critical condition at Stanford Hospital. She said she left her body and looked back and saw our mom kneeling at her bedside. Mom was begging *God* to save Janie's life. My sister said, "A voice told me it wasn't my time. I experienced *total peace* while in this state."

In January, I had a visitation dream from my Uncle Paul. He had crossed over several years before. He loved Janie dearly. *Uncle Paul gave me a wallet with fifty dollars in it. He told me to give it to her for the trip.* As I came out of the dream, I knew she wouldn't be here much longer. My heart felt such sorrow for her.

I returned to care for her the last two weeks of her life. She had been on hospice for a year. By the time I arrived, she was bedridden and semi-comatose. It had been three months since our mom's death. Her dying process was quite similar to Mom's. She struggled until the last few days.

As her lungs filled with mucus, she was gasping, choking and starting to panic. I prayed for help, and a calm came over me. We sat her upright in the bed, and I began to coach her. I said, "Janie, be calm. You know how to do this. Everything is fine and normal. Relax and breathe deep." She visibly relaxed and took several very deep, slow breaths. Even though her lungs were full of mucus and breathing deep was impossible, she managed to experience *deep breath*. Raunell and I felt we had witnessed a miracle.

After this, her struggled breathing was diminished. She started breathing erratically and there was a loud grunting for days. It was as if she wanted to speak and open her eyes, but she absolutely could not. The last day, she got very calm and her last breaths were extremely soft and so sweet. It was like she was blowing out a candle. She had given up the lifetime of effort it took for her to get through each and every precious day.

During this last critical week, our cousin Gerry, also a hospice nurse, came for the day. Together, we decided to go to the funeral home and make final arrangements. We both knew it would make a difference in stress levels after Janie expired. It was a special day, and we made it very personal. I deeply appreciate my cousin for supporting me through the experience. I felt very loved.

I was emotionally crushed and exhausted after the intense days of caring for Janie. As they wheeled her body out, I finally broke down. I said, "And there's a life," as I choked back my sobs. In that moment, I was acutely aware of the gripping, poignant knowledge of how temporary this life is … flooding my heart.

God has graced me with the ability to be strong in the face of death. I have found the end of life to be a very intimate and spiritual time. It is an honor to assist this birthing into the next life. End of life care for my close family members has been both my biggest challenge and greatest reward. I admit it has taken all the courage I can muster.

Janie comes to me in dreams as a free and happy spirit. She is always doing spins and summersaults! I can see that she is delighted to be free of her earth body. Her happiness and glee are obvious. I often sense her by my side always observing and supporting me.

My youngest sister and I went to say goodbye to her body on the cremation day. She looked so lovely just like a fairy-tale princess. She was fifty-two. Her life was an example of bravery and optimism. She remains a true demonstration of love manifested.

A portion of her ashes were divided between her favorite places, Yosemite National Park and the Monterey beach. A crypt at the cemetery holds the remainder. In lieu of a service, we composed the story of her life and sent it to all who knew and loved her. We included a candle and sea shells and asked each loved one to light their candle and send Janie love and prayers. It was an honor to share this life journey with my strong, loving sister.

CHAPTER 23

Father Dharma

Humor is an affirmation of dignity, a declaration of man's superiority to all that befalls him.

~Romain Gary

At the time of my Pisces birth, my father was a medic in the Navy. He was stationed on a naval ship serving in the Korean War. He suffered much trauma during his naval experience. His first assignment was an exercise beyond the Golden Gate bridge where his ship was rammed by another vessel. The navy ship, the USS Benevolence, quickly sank and many of his mates drowned. This trauma, plus the war time suffering he witnessed, left him with a profound sense of sadness. I'm certain these experiences contributed to his lifelong challenges with depression. He first held me when I was nine months old.

My father remained an enigma to me until middle age when we became very close. I felt this awkwardness was largely due to our lack of bonding in those critical first months of life. I always believed he just didn't quite know what to think of his new baby girl. In spite of this, I loved him deeply while longing for more affection on his part. He was a good provider and made certain I had success skills for use in adult life.

The first time I remember feeling emotion from him was the day he had taken all the kids on the ranch for a ride in his open jeep. I was sitting on an oil drum in the back, when he hit a bump, and I fell out onto the road. As the jeep sped down the road, I remember laying there wondering when he would realize I was gone. The other kids summoned his attention. He tenderly retrieved my bleeding body and drove me home to my mother. As he cradled me in his arms, he was crying and shaking. I felt his fear and guilt over the situation. A demonstration of his love was what I desperately craved. The truth is, for much of our life together he was emotionally unavailable for intimacy.

My Dad was known for his intelligence and natural curiosity about everything. His friends called him *Mr. Science*. He was a voracious reader and a man of many talents and interests. He was highly educated. Dad struggled much of his life with AUD (alcohol use disorder). This seemed to be an important and challenging part of his life's journey. He definitely considered himself to be a family man.

I'll fast forward to my father's life after my mother and sister died. He relied heavily on his remaining three children to support him emotionally. Taking care of my mom, in her degenerating condition, had taken quite a toll on him. We observed his depressed state and confusion over what would come next for him. This was his *dark night of the soul*. He decided to try an extended stay with my brother in Southern California. This seemed a good plan at the time.

Dad's spirits lifted. For a period of time, he seemed almost ecstatic. We would eventually discover that his new-found euphoria was for a very sinister reason. He had gotten involved in an intricate internet scam which in the end cost him his pride, self-confidence, and a significant amount of money. I helped him unravel the situation. His drinking had gotten out of control, and he ended up in a rehabilitation center. I told him I knew many seniors had been conned into believing in these criminal internet activities. I supported him throughout the crises.

My father's therapist met with us both. His advice was for my dad to live with family members. He clearly stated, "Your mental state is too weak for you to ever think about living alone again." By this time, my brother and sister had contributed greatly to his life. My dear, unselfish husband invited him to come live with us in Oregon. My dad said he wanted to give it a try. He had just turned seventy-eight. We focused on all the fun we could have together. The three of us liked to camp and fish. This was an opportunity for him to have a new life. Eventually, he decided to stay with us. We helped him sell and liquidate his home in California. My husband and I made every effort to involve him in all aspects of our life.

What we loved the most about him was his sense of humor. He saw the funny side to every situation. This demonstrated to me that love and laughter are closely connected. His sense of humor was a never-ending gift and source of entertainment. There was laughter in every day.

I did insist on an agreement. There would be no substance abuse if he lived in our Oregon home. He was willing to live under these terms, and he did his best to live up to that promise.

I took care of his escalating medical needs. The alcohol abuse had adversely affected the health of his heart. Dad had developed congestive heart disease. We agreed that our time together would be an opportunity to get to know each other better. He desperately needed all the support we could give him.

Over time, his mental health stabilized, and his confidence returned. The three of us had an enjoyable and enriching life. Dad and I conquered the years of awkwardness. We became very close emotionally and spiritually. He lived with us for the better part of seven years. The last three years of his life we lived in the Palm Springs area. He enjoyed the move and change of environments.

His health began deteriorating. I nursed him through; a broken leg, broken hip, pacemaker surgery, and many hospitalizations for heart procedures. We certainly kept busy with all those doctor visits. He had total confidence in my ability to handle his affairs at all levels. With fortitude, my dad always did his part to overcome any physical challenges. He remained as independent as his health would allow. My sister now lived down the street from us. She was able to spend more quality time with him as well.

I began having dreams of his passing about a year before it happened. During the last year, he gradually got weaker. The cardiologist informed us there was nothing else that would help his condition. He said, "Go home and enjoy your life."

My dad admitted, "Honey, I'm wearing out."

I said, "I understand, Dad. We will get through this." Knowing I was curious, he shared many of his thoughts and experiences as his end of life drew near. We openly discussed the next life. He was a skeptic, but as the time drew near, he began to have his own metaphysical awareness of his life.

I asked his doctor to sign him into hospice. Dad said he wanted to die at home, and he did not want to go to the hospital again. The physician was on board with the timing of this decision. His shortness of breath was getting more pronounced. We signed him into hospice and procured all the medications and equipment needed for his home care. There was quite a period of trial and error figuring out the best treatments to manage his symptoms. The added expertise of hospice support was once again invaluable to me.

The stages of his illness progressed weekly. By the third month, we could see he was getting close to the end of his life. He remained mentally alert and coherent until the night he died. He always expressed his gratitude for all that we contributed to his care. Over the years, Dad supported us in any way he could. My husband was an angel during my dad's time with us. He and Dad were good friends and had much in common. Leon never complained, even though my dad's needs became the center of our life for many years.

I expressed to Dad, "Death will not take away the love we have for each other." He agreed whole heartedly. One day he had an experience which he was anxious to share. He said he was sitting quietly in his chair when a force of energy surrounded and filled every part of him. He said he felt totally healed as if he could run a race! He described a state of total bliss. After a few moments, the feeling passed.

He also said that there was a man in his room who stayed with him all the time. I asked if he knew this man. He did not recognize him. I suggested perhaps it was his guardian angel here to support him through his transition to the next life. My father was not one for imaginative thoughts. He insisted the awareness of this spirit was very real.

I asked Dad if he sensed my mother close by. He told me she was getting closer every day. *He had a dream that my mom was waiting for him in a motorhome. When he got in, he told her they could go anywhere and stay as long as they liked!* It was a very happy dream for him.

I stayed in his room his last two weeks. He lived in our casita. I spent the night because he began to have more anxiety, and I was afraid he would fall. I knew his weak heart was not getting enough oxygen to his brain now. This state was quite distressing to him. He was comforted to not be left alone. My sister also helped give me some relief.

Raunell had a dream at this point. *Dad was in a house with her. It was perched on the top of a hill and inside there was a staircase to Heaven.*

The same week, I dreamt of Dad: *He looked smaller, like his energy and presence was diminishing. He came to me in another dream and put his hand on my leg and patted it with great love and reassurance. He said, "Everything is going to be fine."*

Alysia and Sam had each spent a quality weekend with Dad. I called my brother and he flew in with my nephew. This was their opportunity for closure. There was much laughter, story-telling, and a heartfelt good-bye.

Dad told me he didn't feel like he belonged here anymore. He said he didn't recognize the room he was in. I could tell he had one foot in each world now. For a week, it seemed he was just coming and going. For days, his head was itching intensely.

I requested a catheter be inserted in the hope he wouldn't expend priceless energy getting out of bed. He was getting more distressed by his mental state. He had developed sundowner's syndrome the last week of his life. As evening approached, he would get quite confused for a couple of hours until sleep brought relief. This was quite unsettling for him.

He told all of us he was ready to die. He insisted I take him to the bank to cash in his IRA. He wanted to divide it up before his death. I barely got him in and out of the bank before he collapsed. His life force was weakening daily. Fortunately, we had a wheelchair. We had open discussions regarding the handling of his affairs. I knew these conversations gave him a sense of completion.

The morphine did help to ease his difficult breathing. The hospice charge nurse discussed increasing his morphine dose. This was in light of the fact that his suffering had increased. There was nothing left but more suffering. Giving up food and drink will also accelerate the process of dying. My father insisted that he wanted no more nourishment and was certain that he was quite ready to take the next step. He was anxious to increase the narcotic dosage as well.

That very night, as I put him to bed I expressed to him, "I love you so much. Thank you for being such a good dad."

He answered, "I wanted to be." We kissed, and he told me, "I love you *so much.*" He lay there and reminisced some of his life living in a small town. I began the higher morphine dose, and he never regained consciousness. He immediately slipped into a deep sleep.

During the night, I prayed and meditated. *I had a vision of the veil becoming very thin and eventually disappearing. I then saw crystal clear infinite space and his spirit gently floating into it. It was a lovely, peaceful transition.* He was gone by early morning with my sister and husband at his bedside. He waited for me to slip out of the room.

He died peacefully with the knowledge that his affairs were in order. He was ready to start the next adventure. He said it was strange not having anything to look forward to in this life. Our relationship was fulfilled. We left no stone unturned. He consciously crossed over with all the growth and awareness he could squeeze out of this life.

My husband and I were transporting his ashes to Central California for internment with my mom's remains. We were telling stories about Dad. Amazingly, the windshield wipers took one spontaneous swipe for no known reason. He was with us. It is not unusual that spirits can manipulate electricity, and we knew this was our sign. My sister had asked for a sign, from the other side, and her cell phone alarm went off three times without being set.

Leon sang *One More Day*, this time at my dad's graveside. This was Dad's request. He did not want a service unless the entire family could gather for it which was not possible.

After the cemetery burial, we went to breakfast. I clearly heard him say to me, "***Now, get on with your*** *life*." Spoken like only a dad can command! Leon and I drove to beautiful Banff National Park in Alberta, Canada. As we entered the park, I was marveling at the natural beauty of the mountains and lakes and I heard my Dad say, ***"Now that's more like it!"*** It seemed he was with us on the journey.

I experienced an important realization with the death of my father. Over the years, I chose to stay present for every need he presented with. We each did our part to create an intimate, loving relationship. I had no regrets, and this brought me peace and an accelerated experience of healing. My relationship with him often stretched me and provided many opportunities for spiritual growth.

To close out your life consciously is quite an accomplishment. I respected him for having the courage to stay present for the entire experience. He never lost his wit and was able to find humor in all that happened, even at the end. I am grateful for the lessons sharing his last chapter provided. He is truly a forever love of mine.

CHAPTER 24

My Brother ... My Friend

***Being brother and sister means
being there for each other.***

~Unknown

Growing up, my brother Kim was my best friend. Our childhood revolved around each other. He was named after a Korean boy my dad befriended in the war. We were just eighteen months apart. I was the older sister who probably felt displaced at his birth. I was bossy and dominating with my little brother. He loved me nonetheless. He was the introvert and I am quite the opposite. His confidence and pride in me was part of our life script.

Our days were filled with; adventures, cousins, camping, pets, church and life on a ranch. We experienced great times together as children. Our opposite personalities created harmony in our brother-sister love. I was groomed to be the family caretaker, and I always looked after him. As a result of this dedication, I worried incessantly over his welfare. This anxiety followed me throughout my life.

As we aged, life became more complicated. From junior high on, Kim found many rebellious ways to disappoint my parents. He was habitually dishonest, a glitch in his psyche. My mother always defended him. My father, in his frustration, would punish him severely. Often, these abuses were during times of my father's alcohol use. As a result, I was fearful of my father and constantly worried about my brother. He became a heavy drinker and smoker as an adolescent. Kim openly wore the shadow for the rest of the family.

Over the years, we remained connected. Other than our history and love of family, we had little in common. Often, he sought out my support and advice when life threw him a curve ball. It was no surprise when he asked me if I would be willing to serve as his durable power of attorney for his health care. In the event he could not speak for himself: He made it very clear he did not wish to be kept alive if his quality of life could not be maintained. Many years after our conversation, he did in fact become unable to speak for himself.

The last time I spoke to him, he phoned and asked me if my heart was healing from the death of our father. I told him I missed Dad yet was settling nicely into my life without him. I was relieved he wasn't suffering any more. I imagined Dad was fishing with his buddies on the other side. It would be only a short time later my brother would be faced with his own serious health crises.

It was September. Leon and I were on an Alaskan cruise. Both of us had looked forward to this trip for the entire year. We were totally immersed in the mesmerizing, rugged beauty of Alaska's vast landscape. My brother loved Alaska, so it was fitting to spend the trip with him on my mind. The first port we came into my phone lit up with many messages.

My brother was residing in Utah. He had been taken to the hospital with classic heart attack symptoms. Tests revealed a severe aortal dissection. When the surgeon told my brother how serious his condition was, Kim asked that I be called. Unfortunately, I was out of cell range and was not able to have that last conversation with him. He began to send me daily, telepathic messages. This heart condition usually results in sudden death. Miraculously, he made it to the hospital in time to have a ten-hour surgery for aortal repair. The surgeon said it was the worst dissection he had ever seen. It went all the way into the carotid artery and down into the abdomen. My sister and my son flew to Salt Lake City right away.

I decided to stay on the cruise. I knew that I would be needed later. I checked on his progress daily. Each morning, I would be aware of his love encircling me, just as he had given those tight hugs when we were children. He whispered in my ear, *"I love you Sis."* Day after day, there was no change in his physical status. I had a strong feeling he was not going to survive this crises.

He did not wake up. It was agonizing for the family to sit there for hours encouraging him to come back. The doctors kept giving the family hope. As days turned to weeks, the likelihood for any decent recovery waned. In the immediate post-operative period, the doctors focused on the withdrawal from alcohol and cigarettes that would stress his body. They intentionally kept him heavily sedated. His conditioned steadily worsened.

I flew to Salt Lake City two weeks after his surgery. I was reminded of my sworn duty to speak for him now. My nephew was also named on the document. When my brother fell ill, he had been the happiest I had ever seen him. He was enjoying life with his fiancé, his children and grandchildren. A wise person once said, "Life is what happens while we are making other plans." (unknown source) He had been packing up for a camping trip in two days. Looking back, he had been struggling with his breathing and energy for some time.

The neurologist evaluated him. After testing, she told us he had experienced an embolism shower. His brain was full of blood clots. His brain stem was intact, but there was little brain activity. I observed his condition in the Intensive Care Unit for three days. My third day with him, he responded to my voice and made eye contact. He did this more than once in a five-minute period. We became hopeful, praying he was coming out of the coma. Unfortunately, this was his last response to a command. I felt he was trying to let me know he was aware of my presence. He promptly fell back into an unconscious state.

Soon after, his colon stopped working. I talked to every nurse who had taken care of him. I spoke candidly with his doctors. They were planning on taking out the breathing tube, putting in a tracheal tube, and sending him to long term care. I was horrified. The day he looked at me in the Intensive Care Unit, the doctor took him off the respirator to see if he would breathe on his own. They had to reinsert it twenty minutes later. He told me that my brother could not live without the respirator. I knew Kim would never forgive me if I allowed him to stay on life support. Long term care facilities are not a pleasant experience. This would mean more suffering for months to years. He was now showing signs of deeper coma.

I was reminded of a long-ago conversation with a very wise and spiritual woman. She phoned me after James died. These were her words: "Honey, I am so sorry for your loss, and I want to share one truth with you. There are things *worse than death*. You will recover. An entire life lies ahead of you, and you are loved." I never forgot that sage wisdom.

I knew for my brother, existing in long-term care would be a fate *worse than death*. This helped me see the situation clearly. I had tucked that conversation in my heart to be retrieved when needed. Now was the time.

I asked the doctors if it was too soon to consider taking him off of life support. His physicians seemed relieved to have this option put on the table. They agreed it was a reasonable choice. Making this decision was the most stressful thing I have ever had to do. I had experienced the agony of discontinuing cardio-pulmonary resuscitation with my first husband, but this was different.

I knew in my heart what my brother wanted. I had conversations with him in my mind. He told me he loved me … He told me he was trying … Eventually, he told me to let go. I had serious and honest conversations with my brother's fiancé and two of his adult children. At first, his daughter was reluctant. Understandably, she wanted to give him more time to wake up. After careful observation, we all realized he was shutting down. Recovery was not going to happen. It seemed cruel to keep him alive. He showed obvious signs of suffering. It was obvious, his body made the decision for all of us.

I prayed about it. I became resolute in my responsibility to once again look after my younger brother. One night, I had left his room for a break. When I returned, he looked different, and his color had changed. I commented about it to Dana. She said she felt his spirit leave his body.

As a family, we decided to take him off of life support. We were doing our best to follow his written instructions. We would allow him to go to the next life the following night. He had been in a coma for well over two weeks.

The hospital chaplain asked if she could come and pray with us before the respirator was removed. We invited her in and made a circle joining hands with my brother. His son Kris, began with a prayer for his father. There wasn't a dry eye in the room. Next, the chaplain prayed a deeply powerful, magnificent prayer of thankfulness and protection. The room was filled with the energy of the *Holy Spirit*. It was actually palpable! We were all lifted up. The platform was perfect for a good journey. We each gave him permission to cross over. My heart felt fractured, yet I was at peace.

I insisted that the proper medications be administered to him. I did not want him to suffer in his dying. I was reassured by the staff. I had assisted several close family members in their hospice assisted deaths but never in the hospital. The respirator was removed. He was given morphine and other drugs to ease his passage.

He soon began choking. He opened his eyes and was struggling to breathe and in a panic. I was horrified. I summoned the nurse and insisted she medicate him further. She administered all that she was allowed to give. After about ten minutes, he settled down into a more controlled breathing pattern. We watched the monitors as his oxygen levels steadily dropped. His children held him as he crossed over. We all told stories of his life and love. We supported him as his body shut down. His kids played two of his favorite songs. After he died, we sat with his body for a long time; shared more stories, laughed and cried. His son said, "That was the best and the worst experience of my life." I felt honored to be present and help hold the space for the family.

He was sixty-four and died four days before his birthday. I was relieved that he was free of suffering. I was also devastated to lose my brother. I am thankful that he was able to leave his body clean and sober. I felt guided and protected through the entire traumatic experience. Even so, I was tied up in knots and felt incredibly stressed.

The Intensive Care nurse told me she had to notify the donor organization of his death. She said they would be calling soon. I was not familiar with the procedure. My brother had stated in his will that he wished to be an organ donor. They called and asked for his corneas. The family consented. Later that night, a team came and surgically removed his eyes, replacing them with prosthesis. It was his wish to be cremated. Before that would happen, my niece wanted her children to see his body in order to say goodbye. We left instructions with the funeral home to prepare it for viewing later that day.

During the time he was leaving this earth, Kim's three-year-old grandson was upset because there was a man outside his bedroom door! My sister had returned home to California. She felt his presence. He told her to take care of herself. He also conveyed that he was angry and upset about leaving his small grandsons. They were his pride and joy.

The next day, my niece and her family, Dana, and I all met at the funeral home for one last goodbye. The five and three-year old told Grandpa they loved him. It was heart wrenching but so important because they hadn't seen him since before his hospitalization.

My nephew took the money left in my brother's wallet and bought gifts for the grandsons. No doubt my brother put the thought in his mind. He put them in the back seat of my brother's truck and told the boys Grandpa had left them. They were thrilled. Such a thoughtful gesture.

I spent the next few days being as much support to the family as I knew how to be. I helped with settling his financial affairs, etc. I kept hearing my brother's distinctive voice telling me, *"Thank you."* I listened for any thought transference to come my way. A few weeks later, he messaged me that it was *"great"* where he was.

The day after Kim's death, his son felt his presence and heard him say, *"I'm very proud of you, Son."*

A few days later, my daughter was jogging and listening to music, and the song *Blackbird* began playing repeatedly. She felt it was related to her uncle.

Black bird singing in the dead of night
Take these broken wings and learn to fly
All your life
You were only waiting for this moment to be free
Black bird fly, black bird fly
Into the light of the dark black night
Black bird singing in the dead of night
Take these broken wings and learn to fly
All your life
You were only waiting for this moment to arise.
~The Beatles

The next night, Alysia was sleeping with ear plugs in. She relates this experience:

"I was awakened to the loud chirping of a bird. There are no such sounds on the twentieth floor of my building. I felt my uncle's presence. I could see in my mind a small boy of about five. He had a crew cut, rolled up jeans, and very definite white socks. I knew this was my uncle, by the description. He asked me to tell my mom thank you. He also wanted me to tell my aunt to take good care of herself. I summoned my angel, asking her to take him. I saw an energy take him by the hand and lead him to the next life. He was happy to go and seemed quite energetic, a small boy who was excited to start his new adventure."

Alysia was the open channel that night.

The doctors surmised that the years of alcohol abuse, smoking, and hypertension had caused the condition which was his demise.

My brother had a troubled life in many ways, yet he was dedicated to his children. He experienced unconditional love through fatherhood. Kim loved and adored his fiancé. Although he had much living left to do, he left this earth fulfilled.

Through his loyalty, generosity, and kind spirit, he taught me about love. I was grateful to be able to help facilitate such a sudden and difficult circumstance. I was greatly relieved to be able to hear him the entire time. I am blessed to have the knowledge that loved ones are always close.

I have come to believe that phenomenal insights are possible when we love. There is great comfort and peace in knowing that life and learning continue beyond the veil. Love unleashes the potential for healing, has no boundaries, and can allow us to have a peek at wondrous things.

CHAPTER 25

Powerful Perspective

Barn's burned down, now I can see the moon.

~Masahide

What a great school room this life is. The manner in which love weaves its mysterious ways into our experience continually amazes me. I try to listen for the path my heart wants me to follow. This has often not been the easier way.

Within the raw emotions triggered by loss lie the alchemical seeds for transformation. If we call upon our strength and courage, our *Higher Self* assists us in seeing our world with new perspective and wisdom. As we release our dreams, it becomes necessary to refocus our vision for a different tomorrow. Choosing to live in the present moment helps us stay centered and grounded.

I've learned that by sacrificing the things I have made a god of, I am more able to know *God*. As I shine a light on my shadow, it becomes clear that fear in its many forms will block my awareness of the *Divine*.

When I survey the landscape of my life, it is obvious that each steep and rocky climb served a critical purpose in my spiritual evolution. This has helped to define my journey. I realize the most effective survival tool is a belief in my own strength and *God* given power.

Humility is required to create an atmosphere for intimacy. It is useful to remember that we recognize in others what we hide from ourselves. All roads lead back to the self. Different directions simply bring a variety of lessons.

Investing in friendships and building a support system has been an important endeavor to insulate me against the uncertainties of life's dramatic changes. Friends decorate my life, bring joy, and add balance to my journey on earth. The safety net they provide feels like a true miracle in a time of need. Family is forever and having a committed one has been a true blessing.

Getting to know myself and my passions has given me direction during times of uncertainty. Unresolved emotions are like skeletons in the closet.

When loved ones move on, we find our own life review takes place. This is an opportunity to resolve unfinished business and is a powerful time to seek professional guidance. Issues can be faced that will be on the surface. Releasing trapped emotions facilitates living in the present. Journaling is another tool for processing. It has taken me within and helps me keep moving forward.

I have the will to create my world and refocus my perception of circumstances. I can be optimistic in the face of loss and trauma. Knowing I always have choices keeps me from being a victim.

The Twelve Step philosophy has taught me the only step I need take is the next indicated one. Life can truly only be lived *one day at a time*. I have everything I need in any given moment to survive. Transitions are uncomfortable and often confusing. When I don't know which way to go, I can patiently wait for *Higher Guidance* to take me by the hand.

Difficult relationships have given me grand opportunities to practice spiritual principles. The teachings of great masters and guidance of mentors and unseen helpers has given me the working principles needed. Often, life's teachers manifest through distressing circumstances and in elaborate disguise.

Surviving grief has taught me; to honor my feelings, practice gratitude, trust life, and listen to the deep inner voice of my *Higher Self*. I know that grief is triggered whenever life does not turn out the way I wanted or expected. Losses come in many sizes. A persevering commitment to sit with the pain of grief has transformed me into a deeper and stronger spirit. Grief is a process and is definitely unpredictable. Each wave of grief mirrors the happiness once shared.

Death can be slow and laborious or quick like lightening. It is an important stage of our growth and evolution. Preparing for it helps us gain peace through closure. This sets the stage for our transition to the next life and can be an important gift we have the power to leave to our loved ones.

My salvation has been, in part, to be a good receiver. Asking for what I need and delegating to those who offer their assistance is extremely helpful. Life sends love and support in the form of friends, helpers, and synchronous events.

We are here to assist each other on the journey. Each difficult challenge and lesson has helped prepare me to support another and pay it forward. I have been given many opportunities to help others navigate through the frightening early days of loss.

I am able to appreciate more fully my current wonderful life because of my past challenges. I find that true happiness is wanting what I have. Being willing to forgive is a continual powerful teacher which clears the way for miracles to happen.

Sometimes, the most powerful gift you can give to one who is suffering is to have the courage to simply show up. Being present is a way of humbly listening. It is of great comfort and is a true act of compassion.

Co-dependency is not love but fear manifested. Buddha taught: "The greatest protection in all the world is lovingkindness." I know I must give that gift first to myself before extending it to others. I am not my body nor am I my wounds.

I have always been curious about *unexplained phenomena*. By allowing and listening, the heavy cloak of grief has always been lifted from me. This has been replaced by peace and an understanding of the continuum of love and life's cycles.

I know that my heart has a mind of its own. It sometimes defies conventional values and wisdom. There is no logic in love. When the heart speaks … pay attention. My ability and decision to love has been my greatest gift and spiritual teacher. I've learned to pray for *God's Will* which is the voice of my own *Higher Self*. I ask for the ability to carry it out. I can only hear this voice if I continue to work on my ego.

Believing that insight is more important than logic, I pay close attention to guidance in dreams, meditation, and meaningful coincidences. This helps me feel connected to my *Source*. The channels are in place at birth, yet we must practice allowing the gifts to manifest. There is a teaching that says when you feel enthusiastic, you are going in the right direction. I do my best to stay aware of this positive emotion.

It is my experience that the door between worlds is wide open following a loved one's transition. It is a time to listen and be aware of opportunities to connect. Through our senses, the spirit world can communicate with; sound, sight, electricity, thought, smell, or nature to name a few. We also have a sixth sense for receiving messages. Love keeps the channels open. Death is the great equalizer. Our loved ones are only a wisp of air away.

There comes a time to finish grieving. Life always calls us back into its rhythm. It often takes unflinching courage to move on. I believe our loved ones can feel our grief. There seems no benefit to prolonged suffering. I wouldn't say grief has become easier with experience. I have learned that without regret, the cycle of grief is shortened. Making peace with change is required. It is possible to embrace both our new life after loss as well as celebrate our loved one's life and transition to their next adventure.

CHAPTER 26

More Stories from the Edge

Open your heart and you will open your eyes to a new way of seeing.

~Sanaya

On my last two birthdays, *I was visited in lucid dreams by all of my loved ones from across the veil. They came bearing gifts, smiles, and reassurance. I was immersed in unconditional love and blessings.*

These precious spirits are always close. Two different reliable sources have recently shared with me shocking yet comforting experiences of seeing an apparition of their loved one shortly after their passing. There are numerous accounts of this type of brief visitation.

I am reminded of a patient who confided that her mother died when she was twelve. On her wedding day, she was enveloped in the scent of her mother's unusual perfume. Feeling her loving presence meant so much to this bride.

My daughter had a garden wedding on the island of Kauai. At the close of the ceremony, a double rainbow appeared. We knew she was being sent a message of *Divine* love and blessings from the two fathers who had crossed the veil. She also felt deep gratitude to have a loving Papa on this earth to walk her down the aisle on her special day.

I worked with a woman by the name of Betty. She came to me in a dream many years after I had last seen her physically. I found it interesting that she looked about thirty and quite healthy. I never knew her at that age. I called another friend to inquire of her. "Betty died a few months ago," Ann said. I then knew I had seen her from the other side. On numerous occasions, I have seen spirits in this form. The open channel often receives the information.

My good friend, Carol, shared her dramatic and prophetic dream: "My twenty-nine-year old husband worked as a logger. I woke up in the middle of the night crying. I told him I had just had a very real dream of him lying in a casket."

He said, "Don't worry about it. I won't live past thirty anyway."

I said, "Don't say that! He promptly went back to sleep. Less than a month later, I got a knock on the door by the police. I was told to go to the hospital because my husband was seriously injured. My parents met me there with the tragic news that Dennis had not survived

a logging accident. I was left widowed with a three-year-old daughter. I will never forget that dream."
~Carol

Ann relates these three stories: "I always had a special bond with my Aunt Eva. She often reminded me that 'health is your first wealth'. As a nurse, I grew to appreciate these words. It had been four days since my aunt passed away, unexpectedly, from a heart attack. I was standing on her front porch with her sister when I looked up and outward to a clear blue sky. I softly murmured, 'Eva, if there is life after death, send me a sign.' Suddenly, the most colorful rainbow I have ever seen shot across the blue sky exactly where my eyes were focused. This will always be a great moment of belief and contentment for me.

I was blessed to have been raised by a father who was a hard-working, good natured, true 'Irish Gentlemen'. It had been about two weeks since his death. My teenage daughter and I were driving home from shopping. The freeway we were on ran parallel to the cemetery where he was buried. As we drove by, I muttered, 'Hi Dad, Hi Grandpa. If there is life after death, send me a sign.' Spontaneously, as the words left my mouth, a bright beautiful rainbow radiated from the sky and landed on the hood of our van.

My puzzled daughter exclaimed, 'What was that?'

I said, 'Oh that was Grandpa saying hello.' It was fitting for an Irishman to send a rainbow.

My mother was ninety-four when she crossed over. She was a kind, generous, caring mother who loved a good laugh. My cousin had purchased a foil helium *smiley face* balloon to place outside our home for those coming over after the Funeral Service. Eventually, I brought the balloon inside the house and placed it in my great room which included the kitchen. Two days later, I was in the kitchen cooking, and I heard the balloon make a crinkling sound. I looked up and watched it break away from the corner cabinet and drift toward the kitchen. The balloon stopped at the edge of the kitchen counter as if looking at me. I said, 'Is that you Mom?' The balloon shocked me by bobbing three times, clearly shaking a 'YES' my way! I found it very fitting considering my mother was a good cook and spent a lot of time in the kitchen preparing meals".
~Ann

My sister experienced a dramatic sign following the sudden death of her boss. She relates: "The church was filled with mourners for my boss's Memorial Service. During the eulogy, all of the lights on the ceiling spontaneously burst, one at a time, each making a loud popping sound, until the church was in total darkness! The service was completed by candlelight."
~Raunell

My close friend, Susan, received her own postcard from the edge. Her husband succumbed to bile duct cancer two weeks prior to this event. She tells this story: "Bob was fifty-six at the time of his death. I started asking for an obvious sign from him. I wanted to know that he could understand and communicate. Bob had a long-standing habit of saying, 'What's up'? He began every conversation with these words when he called me, friends, or his employees at the guitar store. One morning, I went out to the alley to dispose of trash. As I was walking to the back door of the store, I noticed a postcard on the doorstep. It was a large card from the seventies with black felt and white block lettering. The postcard said, 'WHAT'S UP'? I then knew Bob was listening. This was the first of many messages from him." ~Susan

A friend of ours transitioned after a long battle with cancer. His favorite song was *Wings of a Dove*. Knowing I would be interested, his wife phoned me to share this story: "After the funeral home transported his body, I was alone in our home. I sat down in his chair by the large picture window over-looking our beautiful garden. A white dove flew up to the window and hovered there watching me. I had never seen a white dove in our garden before, let alone hovering at the window! I knew it was my beloved husband saying good-bye." ~Gayle

On the wings of a snow-white dove
He sends His pure sweet love
A sign from above
On the wings of a dove

by Ferlin Husky

Jacob, my cousin's son, passed from this life from Hodgkin's lymphoma. He was seventeen. Several weeks later, Jake's mom began to notice various kinds of feathers in random locations both inside and outside of their home. Her mother-in-law gave her a magazine with an article that discussed the appearance of feathers being a way spirits have been known to communicate. Feathers large and small, even piles of feathers, continued to appear over the months and years. One day, an ostrich feather was sticking out of the wall thermostat! This has been a meaningful sign of his presence and their forever love.

Two days after my interview with Elaine, I received this note: She relates, "We arrived home after our conversation regarding the feathers. We had been on a short trip. After unloading the car and doing all the usual things, I went in the house to unpack. One of the first things I put away was the jewelry I had taken on the trip. I keep my important jewelry in a small stoneware box. When I reached for the box, I noticed something laying on top. It was a *white feather*. I used to question how these feathers got to the places I found them. I have even wondered about my sanity. Now I just smile. I find comfort in knowing my son has been here for a visit. I guess this was Jake's way of letting us know he is on the same page of a book that is being written." ~Elaine

Stories from the edge are varied and always appropriate to each circumstance. They can be subtle or shocking. There are many ways spirits intersect with our earth lives. Dream visitations are quite common. These are priceless gifts. Being aware of messages, guidance, and physical signs sent from the next dimension, provides proof of a continuation of our existence beyond this earth body. Life is absolutely a grand mystery to be solved.

CHAPTER 27

In Conclusion

*Do not allow the illusory urgencies of the immediate
to distract you from your vision of the eternal.*

~Elizabeth Kubler-Ross

Living life and observing death has brought me continual opportunities to learn about the glue of the universe, *love*. I have known love as; intimacy, enthusiasm, empathy, gratitude, honesty, sacrifice, endurance, generosity, patience, joy, humility, and forgiveness.

Experience has shown me time and again that beneath and beyond our stories ... ***Love is always the lesson***.

May you listen carefully for the whispers of love that surround you. Pay attention to the synchronous events which manifest as signposts along the way. These reliable and constant forces will guide, guard, and sustain you through each and every season of your life. They promise to help lead the way to peace and enlightenment.

EPILOGUE

Science ... Mind ... Spirit

"The most beautiful emotion we can experience is the mystical. It is the power of all true art and science. He to who this emotion is a stranger, who can no longer wonder and stand rapt in awe, is as good as dead."

~Physicist Albert Einstein

Science and metaphysics have reached a crossroad. More and more scientists and researchers are seeking and finding empirical evidence to document the existence of the mind as separate from the brain. For those seeking this evidence, it is possible to follow the trail that began centuries ago. Many great minds have alluded to their belief in the supernatural. *The Spiritual Brain* by Mario Beauregard & Denyse O'Leary presents a neuroscientist's case for the existence of the soul. It provides a thorough discussion and includes interesting research in the field of neuroscience. The authors examine the religious, spiritual, and mystical experiences of various groups including a group of Carmelite nuns. There are many examples and varying points of view regarding the existence of God and these metaphysical experiences.

In his book *Erasing Death* by Sam Parnia M.D., we are reminded that death is a process. He says, "Today, the question of consciousness, psyche and soul is a completely new area of discovery that, although an enigma, has thankfully become a point of major focus and interest in science." A new field of medicine, *resuscitation science,* is looking at preserving the brain in emergencies as well as what part of us survives death. His book examines the layers of emerging evidence that we are much more than our physical bodies. The stories of patients, who have been clinically dead and then revived, have much to teach us of the afterlife. He states, "... we can be certain that we humans no longer need to fear death."

Dr. Bruce H. Lipton paints a compelling picture for the spiritual component of mankind in his book *The Biology of Belief.* Advances in science are pointing in the direction of the existence of an intelligence in the universe that many call *God.* We now know how strongly our biology is influenced by our beliefs. I am not a scientist ... merely a nurse who gives love and care to ease suffering.

It has become abundantly clear that my life has followed a pattern. I have been given the opportunity, many times, to assist others at the end of their life as they journey to their next adventure. The strength and spiritual guidance I have received has been miraculously timed to perfection. I am grateful to be able to surrender and to be willing to serve the *greater good*.

Personally, I have never found it important to understand, in a scientific way, how it is possible to hear and see with my inner abilities. I humbly remain available for communication and guidance. In other words, I do my best to *pay attention* and to apply the gift of information to my life. Intuitively, I have always simply known that my experiences were *authentic* and that they were encouraging me to become a stronger and more loving human. I believe that when an experience makes life more understandable and joyful for you or your loved ones then it is *Divine* and is a path worth following, always remembering that we are eternal spirits taking a human journey.

Divine Source

It is my heartfelt desire for all who find their way to these stories to know the blessings of; peace, understanding, discernment, encouragement, insight, and an increased ability to walk their higher path. As we each create and live out our personal stories,
may we remember daily that
love is always the lesson.

With gratitude,
Amen

BOOKS THAT HAVE INSPIRED ME

1. *A Course in Miracles*
    by Foundation for Inner Peace
2. *A Woman's Book of Life*
    by Joan Borysenko, Ph.D.
3. *Al-Anon Handbook*
    by The Al-Anon Family Group
4. *Caring Enough to Confront*
    by David Augsberger
5. *Circle of Stones*
    by Judith Duer
6. *E Squared*
    by Pam Grout
7. *Emmanuel's Books*
    compiled by Pat Rodegast
8. *Grain Brain*
    by David Permutter, M.D.
9. *Hands of Light*
    by Barbara Ann Brennan
10. *Healing After Loss*
    by Martha W. Hickman
11. *How to Survive the Loss of a Love*
    by Bloomfield, Colgrove, McWilliams
12. *I Am the Word*
    by Paul Selig

13. *In the Silence*
     by Suzanne Giesemann

14. *Lazaris*
     by Synergy publishing

15. *Life and Teachings of the Masters of the Far East*
     by Baird T. Spalding

16. *Love*
     by Leo Buscalia

17. *Love Is Letting Go of Fear*
     by Gerald G. Jampolsky, M.D.

18. *Man's Search for Meaning*
     by Victor Frankl

19. *Many Lives, Many Masters*
     by Brian Weiss, M.D.

20. *Messages of Hope*
     by Suzanne Giesemann

21. *Mists of Avalon*
     by Marion Zimmer Bradley

22. *Near Death in The ICU*
     by Laurin Belig, M.D.

23. *On Life After Death*
     by Elisabeth Kubler-Ross

24. *Outrageous Openness*
     by Tosha Silver

25. *Peace Pilgrim* in Her Own Words

26. *Proof of Heaven*
     by Eben Alexander, M.D.

41. *The Tibetan Book of Living and Dying*
    by Sogyal Rinpoche

42. *There is a River*
    by Thomas Sugrue

43. *To Heaven and Back*
    by Mary Neal, M.D.

44. *Too Good to Leave Too Bad to Stay*
    by Mira Kirshenbaum

45. *Unbroken*
    by Laura Hillebrand

46. *Unfinished Business*
    by James Van Praagh

47. *Wheat Belly*
    by William Davis, M.D.

48. *Women Who Love Too Much*
    by Robin Norwood

49. *Women's Intuition*
    by Elizabeth Davis

50. *Your Inner Child of The Past*
    by Hugh Misildine

51. *Your Sixth Sense*
    by Belleruth Naparstek

Disclaimer

This is a work of nonfiction. The events are portrayed to the best of my memory. Realizing memory is often selective, I have kept copious notes and journals immediately following each experience related in this book. Some notes and ledgers I have kept for years and some for decades. While all the stories in this book are true, some names have been changed or intentionally omitted to protect the privacy of the people involved. My psychological, physical, and spiritual understanding of life is gleaned from a lifetime of experience through nursing, the written word, mentors, groups, and metaphysical exposure. I have examined and applied these teachings to my life. Direct quotes are noted.

> *Love is our purpose*
> *God is our support system*
> *Rainbow is our password*
> **~Bobby**

79155282R00171

Made in the USA
San Bernardino, CA
12 June 2018